Schöningh

TEACHERS' BOOK

Discover ...

TOPICS FOR ADVANCED LEARNERS

edited by Engelbert Thaler

Our Environment

A State of Emergency?

by Stephen Speight and Karsten Witsch

www.schoeningh-schulbuch.de
Schöningh Verlag, Jühenplatz 1–3, 33098 Paderborn

Druck 5 4 3 2 1 / Jahr 2014 13 12 11 10
Die letzte Zahl bezeichnet das Jahr dieses Druckes.

Umschlaggestaltung: Franz-Josef Domke, Hannover
Umschlagabbildung: © vario images
Druck und Bindung: Media-Print Informationstechnologie GmbH, Paderborn

ISBN 978-3-14-040109-8

Inhaltsverzeichnis

Die didaktische Konzeption

Die Themenheftreihe *Discover* ... richtet sich an Schülerinnen und Schüler der Sekundarstufe II und bereitet in Anlehnung an die Einheitlichen Prüfungsanforderungen in der Abiturprüfung (EPA) und die Rahmenrichtlinien der einzelnen Bundesländer interkulturell relevante, Jugendliche interessierende Themen methodisch-didaktisch auf.

Der Einstieg in das Thema, das in mehrere Kapitel untergliedert ist, erfolgt über eine Doppelseite „Getting started" mit Bildmaterial und einigen Einstiegsaufgaben. Die Texte weisen unterschiedliche Längen auf, sind aber insgesamt nicht zu lang und berücksichtigen verschiedene Textsorten. Reichlich Bildmaterial (Fotos, Zeichnungen, Cartoons, Grafiken, Tabellen, Karten etc.) ist funktional in die Texte und Aufgabenapparate integriert.

Der Aufbau der einzelnen Texte ermöglicht einen klar strukturierten Unterricht mit drei Phasen: *pre*, *while* und *post reading*. *Pre-reading*-Aufgaben führen zum Text hin, rufen das Vorwissen ab und bauen Erwartungshaltungen auf. Der eigentliche Leseprozess wird im Sinne eines *guided reading* durch gelegentliche Lesebeobachtungsaufgaben und (sparsame) Annotationen in den Fußnoten unterstützt. Im abschließenden Aufgabenapparat unter dem Titel „Activities" werden alle Fragen zu thematisch zusammengehörigen Blöcken mit einer kurzen inhaltlichen Überschrift in der Randspalte zusammengefasst. Diese Aufgaben lassen sich den drei maßgeblichen Bereichen zuordnen:
a) Inhalt (*comprehension*)
b) Struktur, Intention, Stil, Sprache (*analysis*)
c) Evaluation, eigene Meinungsäußerung, sprachproduktive kreative Aufgaben (*evaluation and creation*).

Prof. Dr. Engelbert Thaler, Herausgeber

Discover ... Our Environment – A State of Emergency?

Tabellarische Textübersicht

Land and Water

Autor, Text	Inhaltliche Schwerpunkte	Textsorte	Wortzahl ca.
Lucky Earthlings?	• Introduction of some key terms in a text which points out our good fortune in living on a planet with water, air, and large temperate areas	Informational text with a polemic element	148
Kathy Marks: Indonesia Plants 79 Million Trees	• Indonesia is planning to plant millions of trees as a kind of 'antidote' to the wholesale destruction of its rain forests	Newspaper article	253
Midnight Oil: The Dead Heart	• Protest song linking the plight of the Australian Aborigines with environmental issues	Protest song	150
Jim Yardley: China's Giant Dams	• Report outlining the ecological consequences of the Three Gorges Dam project	Reportage	510
Sara Lyall/Elizabeth Kolbert: Greenland: Two Views	• Contrasting articles on the consequences of global warming for Greenland itself (positive) and the world (negative)	Newspaper article/extract from non-fiction book	200/300
Ernest Callenbach: Ecotopia	• A fictional attempt to convert part of the US into an ecological paradise	Extract from a utopian novel	600
Juliette Jowit: Saving London	• An article about the future of London and the long-term effectiveness of the Thames Barrier as water levels rise	Newspaper article	380
Steve Connor: Arctic Sea Ice Is Melting – Fast	• Report on the increasing speed with which arctic sea ice is melting	Scientific newspaper article/graph	440
Elizabeth Kolbert: Floating Houses	• Information about a row of floating houses on the banks of the Meuse in Holland, and what it is like living in them	Extract from a non-fiction book about global warming	245
Stanley Kunitz: The War against the Trees	• Powerful description of tree-felling to make way for a filling station in someone's front garden	Poem	188
Worksheet im Lehrerheft			
Worksheet 1, p. 35	Elisabeth Rosenthal: Fans of Old-Fashioned Lights Defy a Government Phase-Out		

Air and energy

Autor, Text	Inhaltliche Schwerpunkte	Textsorte	Wortzahl ca.
Stephen Speight: Cars, Cars, Cars	• Good and bad aspects of the car, with special reference to the German car industry	Informational and argumentative text with photographs and a cartoon	450
Chris Chilton: A Car-Lover's Lament	• A motoring journalist wonders whether all the safety/economy/anti-pollution features required on modern cars will mark the end of *'Freude am Fahren'*	Article from a respected motoring magazine	350
The Price of Oil	• Annotated graph from a German newspaper showing rises and falls in oil prices	Information in graphic and text form in German	–
Robin McKie: Oil Apocalypse	• Disaster scenario as oil supplies dwindle, followed by a more optimistic view	Newspaper article putting both sides of the case	435
George, it took me 7 days ...	• 'Letter from God' to George W. Bush, criticising his attitude to climate change	Fictional and humorous letter	–
Nicholas Crane: Why We Must Give up Flying	• A well-known travel writer explains why he has decided never to fly again for environmental reasons	Personal statement and cartoon	558
Marillion: The Last Century for Man	• Song text which claims that our wasteful habits mean that man has entered his last century	Song text	200
Worksheet im Lehrerheft			
Worksheet 2, p. 56	The Wind Farm – A Simulation		

Saving the Planet?

Autor, Text	Inhaltliche Schwerpunkte	Textsorte	Wortzahl ca.
The Global Context	• Information about the 'forgotten' pollution from shipping, and an attempt to reduce it	Brief factual introduction	–
John Vidal: Shipping Boom Increases CO_2 Emissions	• Facts about pollution from shipping compared with pollution from other sources	Informational text	165
David Lister: Islanders Turned Green	• Article about a renewable, independent electricity supply for the island of Eigg	Feature article from a newspaper	445
Michael Crichton: State of Fear	• Two extracts from a novel about the dangers of extreme environmentalism	Modern novel with some scientific elements & graphs	290/345
Rachel Johnson: How (Not) to Be Green	• Humorous article about the environmental paradoxes in family life	Newspaper column	250

Elizabeth Kolbert: Spiralling towards Destruction	• A series of extracts focussing on key aspects of the environmental crisis	Extracts from a non-fiction book about global warming	938
News Flashes	• Kaleidoscopic set of brief items on the topic from different sources	Mainly brief news items	–
Worksheet im Lehrerheft			
Worksheet 3, p. 75	Trudie Styler: It Is Not Hypocritical to Fly If I'm Campagning for the Environment		

Klausuren im Lehrerheft	
Klausur 1, p. 78	Danny Fortson: Rock Battery Could Store Electricity
Klausur 2, p. 82	Patrick Barkham: From the Melting Frontline, a Chilling View of a Warming World

Weiterführende Hinweise

Websites

- UK Department for Environment, Food and Rural Affairs, www.defra.gov.uk
- US Environmental Protection Agency, www.epa.gov
- United Nations Environment Programme, www.unep.gov
- Club of Rome, www.clubofrome.org
- Friends of the Earth, www.foei.org
- Greenpeace, www.greenpeace.org

Books

- Brian W. Aldiss: *Greybeard*, Panther Books, St. Albans 1974 (1964)
- L. P. Hartley: *Facial Justice*, Penguin, Harmondsworth 1966 (1960)
- Cormac McCarthy: *The Road*, Vintage, New York (2007) 2006
- Frederic Pohl and C. M. Kornbluth: *The Space Merchants*, Penguin, Harmondsworth 1973 (1952)
- Paul Theroux: *O-Zone*, Penguin, Harmondsworth 1987 (1986)
- H. G. Wells: *Men Like Gods*, London, Cassell, 1923

Films

- An Inconvenient Truth (USA 2006)
- Darwin's Nightmare (F/AU/BE 2004)
- Erin Brockovich (USA 2000)
- The Day After Tomorrow (USA 2004)

About the Chapter Headings

Calvin and Hobbes

Cartoon The Calvin and Hobbes cartoons are popular in many countries. The little boy, Calvin, is usually accompanied by his soft toy tiger, Hobbes, which can come to life, talk to/argue with Calvin, and play with him. Calvin is in some ways very precocious, in others vulnerable and child-like. Calvin's parents can be described as loving but long-suffering, as in the present example.

Unterrichtsempfehlungen

Es ist denkbar, den Cartoon zu Beginn einer Unterrichtsstunde mithilfe einer Folie und eines OHPs (gegebenenfalls Laptop und Beamer) ohne Aufgabenapparat den Lernenden zu präsentieren. Die Beschreibung des Cartoons bietet gerade zurückhaltenden Schülerinnen und Schülern einen Sprechanlass. Nach der Beschreibung sollten die Schülerinnen und Schüler zur Kommentierung aufgefordert werden; Bezüge zu ihrer eigenen Lebenswelt sollten dabei hergestellt werden. Diese Phase abschließend kann die Lehrerin/der Lehrer die ersten Fragen des Aufgabenapparates nutzen, um das Verständnis des Cartoons in der Breite zu sichern. Zentrale Beiträge sollten von der Lehrkraft gebündelt und zur Überleitung genutzt werden. Die „Basics", Nr. 3–5, können in Kleingruppen stichpunktartig auf Karteikärtchen beantwortet werden. In leistungsschwächeren Kursen kann eine kurze Phase der Redaktion durch die Lehrkraft erfolgen, um insbesondere grobe Verstöße in der Zielsprache aufzufangen. Ein Austausch unter den Kleingruppen sollte dann initiiert werden (z. B. durch die Bildung von Expertengruppen), um zu umfassenden Ergebnissen zu gelangen. Vor diesem Hintergrund kann mithilfe der Frage „How has his attitude to the environment been inconsistent – until now?" ein Unterrichtsgespräch den Arbeitsprozess abrunden und beenden. Die Schülerinnen und Schüler sollten dabei angehalten werden, ihre Beiträge durch die Arbeitsergebnisse aus den vorhergehenden Phasen abzusichern.

Solutions

Activities p. 6

1. **What is Calvin worried about?**
   He is worried about the greenhouse effect, and the fact that his parents will be leaving him a much less pleasant planet to live on.

2. **Why wasn't he worried before?**
   He hadn't heard about the greenhouse effect until recently.

3. **How does Calvin explain the greenhouse effect?**
   He says that pollutants are trapping (in) the sun's heat, which will raise the temperature of the earth and melt the polar ice caps.

4. **What aspects of global warming does he mention?**
   Pollutants, rising temperatures, melting ice caps.

5. **Is there anything he hasn't considered?**
   He doesn't know about the CO_2 problem (CO_2 is not, strictly speaking, a pollutant), and he probably doesn't realise that sea levels will rise if the ice caps melt. He prob-

ably just thinks there ought to be ice at the poles as part of the natural scheme of things.

6. **How has his attitude to the environment been inconsistent – until now?**
   He has not realised that being driven everywhere by car contributes to the problem. We, of course, live in a nation which has millions of cars, many of them far from economical. Exhaust gases can be cleaned, but so far there is no way of eliminating CO_2 emissions.

Different sides of the same coin?

About the photos

The photos show various scenes/activities which are involved, one way or another, with the environment, or threats to it. The arrows connecting them were deliberately inserted in a fairly random way, the aim being to demonstrate that there are interconnections between nearly all aspects of the environment – it's basically a single system.

Unterrichtsempfehlungen

Es sollte das ansprechende Bildmaterial auf eine Folie kopiert (alternativ kann das Material eingescannt werden und mithilfe von Laptop und Beamer präsentiert werden) und dem Kurs als stummer Impuls zu Beginn einer Unterrichtseinheit präsentiert werden. Die Schülerinnen und Schüler erhalten somit die Gelegenheit, in der Zielsprache zu beschreiben, zu spekulieren und methodische Strategien zur Bildbeschreibung anzuwenden.
Die ersten beiden Fragen können dann im Unterricht von der Lehrkraft sukzessiv gestellt werden, um ein Gespräch in Gang zu bringen, dessen Ziel eine vertiefende Auseinandersetzung mit den Bildern und die durch die Pfeile zum Ausdruck kommenden Beziehungen ist. Für die Lehrkraft ist von Bedeutung, sich während des Unterrichtsgespräches Notizen zu machen, um tragfähige Schülerbeiträge für eine Bündelung/Überleitung zur 3. Aufgabe zu leisten. Diese Aufgabe sollte im Rahmen einer Stillarbeitsphase schriftlich ausgeführt werden. Einige nach dem Zufallsprinzip ausgeloste Produkte könnten später vorgetragen oder mithilfe eines Whiteboards dem Plenum präsentiert werden. Dabei sollte das Plenum einen „Hörauftrag" erhalten, z. B. hinsichtlich der Schlüssigkeit der Begründungen.

Solutions

Activities p. 7

1. **How far do you accept the links implied by the arrows?**
   Mainly personal views. Some possible student answers:
   - The link between cheap flights and fuel prices is quite strong, because planes use lots of fuel, and as there are so many cheap flights, this leads to fuel shortages and high prices.
   - Energy shortages are not directly linked with global warming, but the fact that we are burning so much fuel is responsible for climate change.
   - Global warming, which causes ice at the south pole and on Greenland etc. to melt at a higher rate than in the past, is directly responsible for rising sea levels.
   - Rising sea levels and desertification are not directly linked. Desertification can be seen as a result of higher temperatures and man-made variations in weather patterns.

2. **Is anything important missing?**
   No cars/trucks, factories, coal-fired power stations, destruction of rain forests ...

3. The earth has been warmer than this before – and colder, of course. Maybe a bit of global warming could be a good thing. What do you think?

Points which students could make:

⊕

- Short sea-routes , e. g. via the north-east passage to Japan, will soon be navigable.
- Chilly parts of Europe may have better weather/be able to grow crops such as grapes.
- Oil and other resources will become available as the ice retreats.

⊖

- Very large numbers of people living in low-lying areas will become displaced persons. This could lead to social unrest/wars in areas they try to relocate to.
- Attractive parts of the world, e. g. Southern France, Spain, parts of Italy, will (and in some cases already are suffering) suffer from severe water shortages/creeping desertification.
- Various problems are arising from melting permafrost in Russia/Alaska and elsewhere (buildings and pipelines sink into the ground, the previously hard surface of the ground turns into mud).

Land and Water

Lucky Earthlings?

About the text

This text by the Editor was written with a view to providing some background information and key terms for dealing with the topic of the book. In particular, it was felt to be important to stress how lucky we are to be living on such a (mainly) temperate planet, with plenty of water, breathable air, etc. We disturb this wonderful state of equilibrium at our peril. Admittedly, our environment has been fairly stable in the past, in spite of the ice ages, but we are moving into unknown territory as temperatures continue to rise.

Unterrichtsempfehlungen

Der Aufgabenapparat kann nicht unmittelbar im Rahmen einer Unterrichtseinheit angegangen werden. In Anlehnung an kooperative Lernstrategien (*think – pair – share*) sollte die *Think*-Phase in den außerunterrichtlichen Bereich verlegt werden und als Hausaufgabe stichpunktartig bearbeitet werden. Die Schülerinnen und Schüler erhalten den Auftrag, in Bezug auf die Aufgaben zu recherchieren, sich Informationen zu beschaffen. Im Unterricht können mithilfe der *Pair*- und *Share*-Phase Ergebnisse ergänzt werden. Ein kleines Quiz kann von der Lehrerin/dem Lehrer durchgeführt und zur Absicherung der Ergebnisse genutzt werden. Diese Vorgehensweise ist zu empfehlen, da die Denkanstöße „Lucky Earthlings?" und der Aufgabenapparat in motivierender Weise auf zentrale Themen des Schülerbuches hindeuten und Neugier wecken sollen. Unter www.learnline.nrw.de/ findet sich eine Vielzahl von kostenlosen Beispielen und Anregungen zum Kooperativen Lernen.

Solutions

Activities p. 9

1. **Comment on the photographs above, with special reference to their environmental implications.**
   - **Arctic landscape**
   Deserted, icy landscape which has probably looked like this for thousands of years – but perhaps for not much longer.
   - **Melting glaciers in Alaska**
   The characteristics of mountainous areas are changing all over the world, resulting in rising water levels, also water shortages as there is less meltwater to supply rivers.
   - **Mountain bikers in Italy**
   At present these mountain bikers are enjoying the wonderful Mediterranean scenery and climate, which, as we have seen, is already under threat from rising temperatures and water shortages.
   - **Traffic jam in Beijing/Peking**
   The explosive growth of the economies in China and India in particular, with parallel rises in energy consumption and pollution of all kinds, is as much or more of a threat to the planet than the 'greedy' economies of the US, Europe, Japan and Australia.

2. **Which American politician has won the Nobel Peace Prize for his environmental activities?**
   Al Gore

3. **How do we know that countries like Denmark were once covered with ice?**
   The countryside was flattened by the ice sheet, and stones/boulders pushed along by the ice have been rounded off by the friction. (The land is still rising slowly in these areas as it is no longer pushed down by the weight of the ice.) Geography specialists can go on to talk about moraines, glacial lakes etc.

4. **What probably happened to the dinosaurs?**
   They probably failed to survive the catastrophic consequences of a major meteor strike.

5. **What is a carbon footprint?**
   This is the fashionable term for the total amount of carbon in all forms emitted by a factory/country/family.

6. **Roughly what proportion of our energy comes from renewable resources?**
   As the figure is changing all the time, students can do a bit of research here. Generally speaking, the figure for most countries is far lower than all the interest in renewable energy would suggest – single rather than double figures, although this is changing slowly in the right direction in most parts of western Europe and elsewhere.

7. **What are greenhouse gases? What is their effect?**
   See the first item on p. 51 of the SB for a detailed explanation. Students should at least know that greenhouse gases in the atmosphere, such as carbon dioxide, prevent some of the sun's heat from being reflected back into space. Without some greenhouse effect, the ambient temperature on earth would be around 0° C.

8. **What do Kyoto and Bali have to do with environmental issues?**
   These were important global conferences which were intended to lead to major improvements on environmental issues. Unfortunately, major players either did not attend, or did not agree to mend their ways. Improvements have been modest, or non-existent.

9. **Who might think a bit of global warming is a good thing. Would they be right?**
   Greenlanders, people living in northern holiday resorts, shipping companies (opening up of new, shorter sea-routes to the other side of the world). They could be right in local terms, but on a global scale global warming is definitely not a good thing.

Land – Use It, Abuse It, Lose It

Text and photo The short text is intended to remind students that rain forests are irreplaceable, and that we only have a finite amount of land to live on, some of which we are well on the way to making uninhabitable. The photo shows the devastating results of turning rain forest trees into charcoal. Note the second row of ovens behind the first. This is destruction on a really major scale.

Background information Charcoal is made by burning wood slowly, without the presence of oxygen. It is used as a fuel, by artists, and for cooking, including grilling, of course.

Unterrichtsempfehlungen

Die Lehrkraft sollte die provokante Überschrift „Land – Use It, Abuse It, Lose It" gut lesbar auf einer Folie dem Kurs präsentieren und ihn damit zu Reaktionen veranlassen. Der kleine Text kann dann in Einzelarbeit gelesen werden. Jeweils eine der vier Aufgabenstellungen sollte auf ein großes Poster geschrieben werden/als Kopie aufgeklebt werden. Danach wird je ein Poster mit einer Aufgabenstellung in eine Ecke des Kursraumes gehängt. Die Lernenden erhalten den Auftrag, in Kleingruppen von Poster zu Poster zu gehen, ihre Antwort stichpunktartig auf den Postern festzuhalten und die Stichhaltigkeit der Punkte in der Zielsprache gemeinsam zu diskutieren. Danach teilt die Lehrkraft den Kurs in vier Gruppen ein, jeweils eine Gruppe erhält ein Poster, deren Gruppenmitglieder sich sämtliche Punkte/Antworten auf dem Poster in ihre Hefte notieren. Als Hausaufgabe muss nun von jeder Schülerin/jedem Schüler eine Überprüfung, Ergänzung und Korrektur vorgenommen werden. In der folgenden Stunde sollte eine Ergebnispräsentation stattfinden, bei der die Lehrkraft moderierend, behutsam korrigierend bzw. nachfragend agiert. Aufgabe 5 sollte für eine den Arbeitsprozess abrundende Diskussion im Plenum Verwendung finden, Aufgabe 6 hingegen als schriftliche Übung/Hausaufgabe erledigt werden.

Solutions

Activities p. 10

1. **Why are the rain forests important? After all, England cut down most of its trees to build ships, and the country doesn't seem to have suffered too much as a result.**
   Points to make:
   - many rare species live in the rain forests
   - absorb CO_2 and produce oxygen
   - erosion takes place when the trees have gone
   - wonderful, irreplaceable variety of life forms, plants and animals
2. **What are the alternatives to landfill sites for disposing of rubbish?**
   - incinerators
   - recycling
   - methane production
   - reducing waste production at source
3. **What kind of crops replace rain forests as a rule?**
   - palm oil, cereal crops mainly for beef production
4. **Can you think of some really major 'earth-moving' and building schemes? What is their effect on the environment?**
   Students should bring in their own knowledge here. Typical examples are new motorways, or in Germany the building of the Fehmarn Belt bridge with associated major earth-moving on land. Open-cast mining is another good example. Effects on the environment are typically destruction of the landscape, people having to move house, destruction of plant and animal habitats.
5. **What might a Greenlander think about global warming?**
   He might be quite pleased – see SB p. 16.
6. **Describe and comment on the photograph below.**
   In the background there are long rows of dome-shaped ovens used for making charcoal. The charcoal-burning operation is clearly on an industrial scale. The logs in the foreground are clearly intended for use in the ovens. As we know that the logs are from trees in the Amazon rain forest, we can consider this as a scene of devastation/a tragic scene. Nothing is growing in this area, which was until quite recently virgin forest.

really cares (about the issue)

- She makes it clear that she is sceptical about the effectiveness of the tree-planting scheme.
- The whole thrust of the article is to make it clear to the reader that this is an important issue/that great damage is being done/and that at present very little is being done to stop it.
- Final sentence makes clear the scale of deforestation compared with transportation, which we know is a major polluter/source of greenhouse gases.

The Dead Heart

Midnight Oil

About the text

It will help students to come to terms with the text if it is made clear to them that the (white Australian) group are singing on behalf of a quite different ethnic group, and that this group, the Aborigines, suffer from severe discrimination as the minority in the country which was once theirs. The angry words in the text are a good example of empathy – making someone else's feelings one's own.

Unterrichtsempfehlungen

Der Song sollte zunächst ohne Text bei geschlossenem Schülerbuch vorgespielt werden (alternativ: als Video präsentiert werden, leicht bei YouTube zu finden). Die Schülerinnen und Schüler sollten sodann Raum für Spontanäußerungen und Kommentierungen erhalten. Die Lehrkraft kann anschließend Aspekte aus den Schüleräußerungen aufgreifen, die auf die zentrale Problematik von „The Dead Heart" hindeuten und diese spiegeln. Das Statement „The speaker clearly sees the environment as a racial issue." sollte mithilfe einer Folie und des OHPs dem Plenum gezeigt werden und die Schülerinnen und Schüler zu Reaktionen veranlassen. Eine Vertiefung sollte in Partnerarbeit erfolgen. Im Sinne der ersten Aufgabe soll das Statement vor dem Hintergrund des Textes auf seine Stichhaltigkeit überprüft werden. Die Ergebnisse können in einem offenen Unterrichtsgespräch ausgetauscht, d.h. verifiziert, modifiziert und falsifiziert werden.

Zur Bearbeitung der zweiten Aufgabe kann der Kurs in zwei Gruppen geteilt werden, wobei eine Gruppe *comments* zu Punkt a und eine Gruppe *comments* zu Punkt b sammelt. Diese sollten von den beiden Gruppen in einfachen Aussagesätze in der Ich-Form formuliert werden. Die Gruppen bilden dann zwei Reihen, stehen sich gegenüber und konfrontieren sich abwechselnd mit ihren Aussagen. Diese Übung kann zügig durchgeführt werden; auch wenn sicherlich einige Aussagen wiederholt werden dürften, kommt die im Song zum Ausdruck kommende starke Polarisierung sehr deutlich zum Tragen. Diese Übung wirkt sich darüber hinaus zielführend auf die Bearbeitung der 3. Aufgabe aus, die schriftlich als Hausaufgabe bzw. im Rahmen einer Stillarbeitsphase erledigt werden kann.

In einer folgenden Unterrichtseinheit sollten die Aufgaben 4–6 auf drei Gruppen verteilt werden (in sehr großen Kursen müssen evtl. gleiche Aufgaben auf mehrere Gruppen verteilt werden). Die Arbeitsphase sollte durch kooperative Lernstrategien gekennzeichnet sein und die Phasen „Think – Pair – Share" beinhalten. Aufgabe 7 sollte von den Schülerinnen und Schülern schriftlich bearbeitet werden, da die Aufgabenstellung in Anlehnung an Klausuraufgaben gestellt ist, wie sie auch im Zentralabitur NRW vorgesehen sind und somit der intensiven Klausurvorbereitung bzw. dem Aufbau von Schreibroutine dient.

Solutions

Activities p. 13

1. **'The speaker clearly sees the environment as a racial issue.' Try to find evidence for this statement in the text.**
   e. g. 'We don't serve your country/king' (ll. 1/2)
   'White man came took everyone/everything' (ll. 4/8)
   '... companies/got more right(s) than people' (l. 26)

2. **List the comments made by the speaker about a) the white man, b) his own people.**
   a) white man
   'White man listen ...' (l. 7)
   'White man came took everyone/everything' (ll. 4/8)
   'We don't need protection/your land' (ll. 18/19)
   'Mining companies ... got more rights than people' (ll. 23–26)
   b) own people
   'We don't serve your country/king' (ll. 5/6)
   'We don't speak your tongue' (l. 3)
   '(we sing) songs' (l. 7)
   'We carry in our hearts the true country ...' (l. 10)
   'We follow in the steps of our ancestry' (l. 12)
   '(don't) know your custom(s)' (l. 3)
   'We don't need protection/your land' (ll. 18/19)
   'We will listen/understand' (l. 21)

3. **Explain the third four-line verse (lines 10–14) in your own words.**
   The speaker is saying that the various violations carried out by the white man are in a sense superficial, because the 'true country' is carried in the hearts of his people, and thus cannot be stolen. Similarly, the link between his people and their ancestors cannot be broken by the white man, who has no understanding of these traditions and no sympathy for them.

4. **Why should anyone treat the fairly distant past as if it is the present?**
   Some points which could be made:
   - The past was a happier time for the speaker's people.
   - They were free – not governed by an alien people.
   - a general feeling of nostalgia
   - To some extent life for the Aborigines was timeless.
   - Their way of life persists into the present to some extent (and in the hearts of the aboriginal people) in spite of modern influences.

5. **Discuss the statement 'Forty thousand years can make a difference'.**
   The timeless life-style of the Aborigines continued for many thousand years in the past until it was disrupted by the white man. They are sure that they will still be around in forty thousand years, but by then the white man may have disappeared from their part of the world. Their lifestyle, with its minimal effect on the environment, may well turn out to be more resilient than white lifestyles, with climate change playing a role (white Australians losing their farms because of drought, high incidence of skin cancers, forest fires destroying white suburbs).

6. **Try to explain the title – and the second reference to the 'dead heart' at the end of the text.**
   We can't know for certain what the speaker means here, but it is credible to imagine that the title suggests that the 'heart' of the Aboriginal people has almost been killed by the white man. Much of the text contains evidence for a kind of mental genocide

destroying the Aboriginal life style (and in many cases actually killing people, taking away their children to be educated like white children, etc.).
However, they 'carry in (their) hearts the true country', so in fact the apparently dead heart is not dead at all, but rather in a state of suspended animation/a kind of coma. This view is confirmed by the last line.

7. **List some examples of non-standard English in the song. Who might speak like this? What effect does this kind of language have on the reader/listener?**
   - singular forms instead of plural, e.g. custom, right
   - omission of pronouns, articles, conjunctions, e.g. '(We) don't serve your country/ king', '(The) white man came (and) took everyone', '(They have) got more right(s) than people'

   Clearly these devices are intended to convey some characteristics of aboriginal English. Various effects on listeners are possible, e.g.
   - There are widespread prejudices against people who do not speak standard versions of languages, so some people might look down on the Aborigines for this reason
   - People who are sympathetic towards the Aborigines could say that it is our language, not theirs, so we should not judge them on the basis of their mastery of English.
   - These abbreviated forms of language also have a kind of primitive strength which standard language may not have.

China's Giant Dams

Jim Yardley

Text and photograph

The photograph shows piles of possessions belonging to poor villagers who have had to move house lock, stock and barrel, as the waters behind the great Three Gorges Dam system rise. Relocation seems to be a fairly arbitrary business. It is unlikely that the villagers will be able to support themselves as in the past when they have resettled.
The text does not go into detail about the reasons for building the dam, so students should be given some brief information before reading the text (and answering the first 'Activities' question below). We can assume that it is intended to control the flow of river water in the gorges, and provide better/more reliable water supplies for large areas of China, which suffers from severe water shortages in some parts of the country.

Background information

The Three Gorges Dam was constructed at a place called Sāndòupíng in the middle of the Xiling Gorge. The reservoir was completed in the summer of 2006, and the water level in the Qutang, Wuxia, and the western portion of the Xiling Gorges has risen steadily. The dam body was finished in 2006 and all of the originally planned dam components of the project were completed on October 30, 2008. In addition to the impacts of the dam on the ecology and people (i.e. the mass relocation of towns and villages) of the region, the dam will also change the scenery of the Three Gorges. Because the water level will be higher, the river will be wider and the mountains will appear lower. Proponents of the dam point out that because the mountains reach several thousand feet above the river, the gorges are still likely to offer spectacular views of the surrounding cliffs, and it should be noted that most riverboat companies that operate in the Three Gorges intend to continue to offer tours of the region. The increase in width of the Gorges will also allow larger ships through the gorges, and it is anticipated that river traffic of all kinds will increase.

Adapted from Wikipedia, www.en.wikipedia.org, 10.05.2009 [07.10.2009]

Unterrichtsempfehlungen

Die Vorbereitung des Textes in Kombination mit dem Foto erfolgt als Hausaufgabe. Die Schülerinnen und Schüler sollten bei der Lektüre des Textes die Lesebegleitfragen am Rand stichpunktartig beantworten.
Vor diesem Hintergrund können in Partnerarbeit die Fragen 1–3 angegangen werden und anschließend umfassend im Rahmen eines Unterrichtsgespräches diskutiert werden. Dabei sollten die Fragen nicht einzeln „abgehakt" werden, sondern unter einer übergeordneten Problemstellung angegangen werden – „Why is it a giant project?"/ „Why can it be called a giant project?" Die Lehrkraft sollte dabei den Kurs motivieren, Antworten und Ergebnisse aus der Partnerarbeitsphase deutlich zu berücksichtigen.
Als Abschluss der Unterrichtseinheit können die Fragen 4 und 5 in Kleingruppen diskutiert werden. Die Lehrkraft sollte sich abwechselnd den Gruppen zuwenden, bei Bedarf moderierend und redaktionell eingreifen.
Abhängig von der technischen Ausstattung der Schule kann die Aufgabe 6 mithilfe eines Whiteboards erarbeitet werden. Der Stilwechsel im Artikel kann visualisiert werden; der zweite Teil der Frage „Where does this happen, and what exactly changes?" durch Notizen am Textrand herausgestellt werden.
Die abschließenden Fragen 8 und 9 fördern die interkulturellen Kompetenzen der Lernenden. Da hier persönliche Stellungnahmen verlangt werden, sollte jeder Schüler/jede Schülerin zunächst in einer kurzen Stillarbeitsphase Gelegenheit haben, seine Position zu bestimmen, bevor es zu einem Austausch im Plenum kommt.

Solutions

Before you read p. 13

... the great dam projects in China also have a lot to do with land. What, for example?
- villages inundated/farming land flooded
- possible social unrest
- man-made geological changes as a result of earth-moving activities, water pressure/ dam-building

While-reading tasks p. 14

What do you make of the two figures quoted for displaced persons (here and in the first paragraph)?
It would be unrealistic for the Chinese authorities to claim that no one was displaced by such a huge project. They admitted to a 'world record' figure, but this was far lower than the actual numbers involved. We can assume that the authorities would be worried about their reputation and possible social unrest if they revealed the true scale of resettlement.

What rhetorical device is used in the last sentence?
This is a clear case of irony. Local officials have (presumably) tried to improve the environment, but people living near the monument built in their honour have suffered a major environmental disaster.

Activities p. 15

1. **Explain the purpose of the Three Gorges Dam scheme in your own words.**
   Points to make:
   - control flow of rivers in deep gorges
   - store vast quantities of water
   - ensure reliable water supplies for towns and farms
   - safer for shipping/larger ships can use the rivers
2. **List some of the 'world record' statistics associated with the scheme. How far do you think the Chinese government is right to be proud of these statistics?**

World records:

- world's biggest dam
- biggest hydro-electric power plant/station
- dirt/earth moved
- stone, steel and concrete used
- people resettled

The Chinese government certainly has the right to be proud of successfully completing a project on such an enormous scale, and for a long time they were only interested in favourable comments/reporting about the scheme.
However, more recently problems of various kinds have begun to come to the surface, but these had not been remedied at the time when the article was written (2007).

3. **Find evidence that the project was not very well-planned in some respects.**
   The scheme has led to:
   - water pollution is some areas
   - landslides
   - silting up of the reservoir floor
   - a man-made earthquake
   - people displaced in far larger numbers than the authorities originally admitted

4. **In what ways is the environment affected by this project?**
   (Students should use their common sense here as well as referring to the text.)
   - The balance of nature, built up over millenia, will have been drastically upset, with unpredictable consequences.
   - The same applies to living patterns.
   - Fertile land has been inundated – the alternative living areas for displaced villagers are often on poor quality land, which means that they cannot live without government assistance.
   - It is quite possible that when things have settled down, the huge lake will be seen as a genuine environmental asset.

5. **How important are individuals for the Chinese planners?**
   Individuals obviously play an insignificant role in the minds of the planners. The planners assumed that people could be moved around like figures in a kind of board game, when in fact there are all kinds of problems associated with resettlement even on a small scale as, for example, in connection with open-cast mining in Germany.

6. **Part of the way through the article there is a sudden change of style and approach on the part of the author. Where does this happen, and what exactly changes?**
   The change comes at line 32. Up until this point, the style is straightforward factual/objective reporting, although the topic changes from outlining the earlier official view, to documenting the response to the various problems which have arisen. After line 32 we have a 'human interest' approach, with the following features:
   - use of direct speech (lines 35–39)
   - use of graphic/emotive/descriptive language, e.g. screams, sickening sensation, earth collapsing, mountain farmhouse ..., buckled, fending off rats (lines 40–44)

7. **Why do you think the author decided to do this?**
   The most likely reason is that he will have wanted to get across the human misery involved in such a scheme when individuals are not taken into account. The three-way trek to the official site of the new village, the return to the old village, and the move to a tented camp after the landslide will all have been traumatic events for the people involved. The transition from reasonably prosperous rice farmers living in a mountain farmhouse (which buckled and was swept away – a truly elemental disaster scenario for anyone), to becoming destitute tent dwellers fighting off rats, successfully brings the human dimension of the scheme home to the reader.

8. What would happen if a project like this was planned in Germany (think in terms of new motorways, airports, etc.)?

Students should be encouraged to find out more about major schemes in their own area as a kind of mini-project. Some points they could try to gather information on:

- consultation processes during the planning phase
- protests
- amount of destruction of natural environment
- effects on future quality of life for local residents (noise and other kinds of pollution, etc.)
- the inevitable threat to rare species
- long-term losses and gains

9. Why do you think reactions would be so different?

The assumption here was that almost any planned major project in Germany arouses hostility from people living near it for the reasons implied above, and there are likely to be long delays before the bulldozers move in – if they ever do. The huge difference between this situation and what happened in China is that here protests are taken seriously, and acted on as a rule/if possible, whereas in China the work just went ahead and people had to (be) move(d) out of the way, whether it suited them or not. We can also assume that the civil engineering aspects of such projects would be conscientiously planned in Germany (although a bridge did fall into the Rhine while it was being built not so long ago!). Business people and local residents are often on different sides in the debate on new motorways, runways, etc., for obvious reasons. The protesters are seen by the planners as an irritation, but their views still have to be taken into account.

Greenland: Two Views

Sara Lyall/Elizabeth Kolbert

Texts and graph

The texts and the graph are intended to help students understand how different views about global warming can be, depending on who is talking, where they are reporting, and what lobby they represent. Here the graph shows very large variations in the past, a consistently much warmer climate fairly recently, but a slight, not necessarily significant decline again, nearer the present.

About Elizabeth Kolbert and her book

Kolbert is an American journalist whose views are read and respected by scientists as well as by the general reader.

"Short, readable and scrupulously objective ... Kolbert's central achievement is to have examined the complex panoply of data surrounding the science of climatology and have presented it in prose as elegant as the facts themselves are stark." (*Times Literary Supplement*) See also p. 51 of the SB.

Unterrichtsempfehlungen

Die Arbeit zu „Greenland: Two Views" bietet sich ganz besonders an, um das individuelle Leistungsvermögen der Schülerinnen und Schüler individuell zu fördern. Hinführend sollte im Plenum zunächst das Diagramm geklärt werden (vgl. dazu auch *The New Summit*, Method Kit: Analysing Statistics). Die beiden Texte „Greenland Goes Green – Again" und „History as Ice-Story" mit den passenden Activities können dann in zwei Gruppen (bei größerem Kursen in vier Gruppen – zwei Gruppen erhalten jeweils den gleichen Text) bearbeitet werden. Da der Text von Sara Lyall leistungsschwä-

cheren Schülerinnen und Schülern entgegenkommt, sollte dies bei der Gruppenbildung von der Lehrerin/dem Lehrer berücksichtigt werden. Eine Ergebnissicherung sollte mithilfe der Kugellager-Methode (*double circle*) durchgeführt werden. Die Methode des Kugellagers eignet sich zum einen dazu, mehr Verbindlichkeit im Rahmen der Gruppenarbeitsphase zu schaffen, da alle Schülerinnen und Schüler die Ergebnisse präsentieren, über sie berichten müssen. Zum anderen kommt sie der Kommunikationsorientierung eines modernen Englischunterrichts entgegen, da die Methode einen sehr hohen Sprechanteil auf Seiten der Schülerinnen und Schüler ermöglicht.
Die Aufgaben 7–9 dienen der Sicherung und Vertiefung. Im Rahmen einer Stillarbeitsphase oder Hausaufgabe sollten sie schriftlich bearbeitet werden. Während die Aufgabe 7 zu einem Fließtext führen sollte, dürfen die Aufgaben 8 und 9 stichpunktartig, skizzenhaft beantwortet werden. Zentral ist bei diesen Aufgaben der Rückbezug zu den Texten, eine anhand der Texte stichhaltige und nachvollziehbare Bearbeitung.

Solutions

Before you read p. 15

What do you make of the graph below – and how do you think the information in it was obtained?
See the first short text above. Some students may know about ice cores as a source of information about temperatures in the past.

While reading tasks p. 16

Why mention the strawberries?
Strawberries are seen as a crop which grows in fairly warm climates (rather like grapes), so it represents a kind of 'climatic milestone' for the Greenlanders to be able to grow them. Even if it's only a few, it's a status symbol for successful gardeners, but not to be taken too seriously.

Why 'as it were'?
The word 'glacially', which can be used to describe the movement of glaciers, is quite often used figuratively to describe any process which takes place extremely slowly. Here the topic is actually used in connection with ice.

While reading task p. 17

Why might this be?
The most likely explanation of thickening at the centre of the ice sheet while it is generally shrinking is that there are heavier snowfalls inland as the result of warmer, damper air as a result of climate change.

Activities p. 17

1. **Describe the history of Greenland's climate from the 10th century to the present day in two or three sentences.**
   From the 10th to the 16th century Greenland was a fairly warm country, inhabited by descendants of the Vikings. During the Little Ice Age which followed, agriculture became impossible and the Norse settlers died out. Recently, however, Greenland has become warmer again, and various crops can be grown for the first time.

2. **Explain how Greenland's farmers regard the present-day warming of their country.**
   They are very pleased that their growing season is longer, and are experimenting with crops which would have been out of the question in the past because it would have been too cold for them.

3. **To what extent are they worried about possible worldwide consequences?**
   They are not worried at all. On the contrary, for them personally the consequences of global warming are seen as entirely positive, at least as reported here.

4. **Summarise the information which is provided by an analysis of the ice cores.**
   Analysis of the ice cores reveals that climate change can take place quite fast. About

12,800 years ago, there was a sudden reversal. A rapid warming phase ended and a new ice age began, which lasted for twelve centuries. Then there was another warming phase, with more rapid change than before. The earlier warm phase was somewhat warmer than the present one.

5. **What do they tell us specifically about the climate in Greenland (and elsewhere on the planet)?**
The effect on the climate in Greenland itself is obvious – warm, cold, warm. The effect on the rest of the world can be calculated fairly accurately from the Greenland data. We can assume, for example, that there will have been a major rise in sea levels as the Greenland ice sheet and possibly the West Antarctic ice sheet melted. We can assume that temperatures elsewhere in the world rose and fell proportionately along with those in Greenland, although there may have been local variations depending on factors such as the Gulf Stream, for example.

6. **What is the most surprising finding, and why should we be concerned about it?**
Students may mention two possible candidates here, either the fact that the climate can change quite rapidly after long stable periods, or the fact that the Greenland ice sheet is shrinking by the huge amount of twelve cubic miles per year.

7. **Outline and contrast the different views expressed in the two texts. Why do you think there is so little agreement between the two authors?**

Lyall	Kolbert
Warmer climate is a good thing.	Rapid warming is dangerous and will lead to rising sea levels.
All kinds of crops can now be grown in Greenland.	(Implied) Major rises in sea levels will be disastrous for low-lying areas and their inhabitants.
local view of climate change	global view of climate change
entirely favourable view based on personal observation/experience	negative, scientifically based view based on research in central Greenland (not near the coast where people live) and elsewhere

The lack of agreement between the two authors/articles depends on the fact that the inhabitants of Greenland take a *local* view, and are naturally pleased that their icy island has become warmer, while Kolbert reports on the consequences of rising temperatures in a *global* context.

8. **Whose side are you on? Try to give reasons for your choice.**
Points which could be made:
for:
- Other cold countries will have a warmer climate, too.
- opening up of new sea routes
- Consequences may not be as dramatic as some people think – not much has happened yet.
- The Baltic could become the new Mediterranean, which would be very good news for Baltic economies.

against:
- The world is moving into uncharted territory. We just don't know what will happen if the world becomes warmer than ever before.
- danger to low-lying islands, coastal areas world-wide
- ecological change on a massive scale, e. g. reduced icemelt water for major rivers and the populations which depend on them
- The mediterranean countries could have very severe and persistent water shortages/danger of desertification.

9. What kinds of material are the extracts taken from? Try to find evidence for your answer in the texts.

Lyall: newspaper article.

- style light-hearted, e.g. the reference to Erik the Red, the material about strawberries, etc.
- use of direct speech
- references to familiar animals and vegetables so that the ordinary reader is not 'blinded with science'
- short paragraphs to keep the reader's interest

Kolbert: popular but scientific book

- use of technical terms, e.g. isotopic, which most readers would have to look up
- objective style, avoidance of sensational elements although the facts are dramatic
- careful formulations, e.g. *much* of what is known, *somewhat warmer*
- long paragraphs, assumption that the reader has a long attention span

Ecotopia

Ernest Callenbach

About the author

Ernest Callenbach is an American author, born in 1929. His career began in the film industry, but he later became interested in what we would now call 'green' issues, particularly sustainability. His best-known work is *Ecotopia*, a word which he is credited with using for the first time.

Unterrichtsempfehlungen

Die Lektüre des Textauszuges „Ecotopia" mit den hinführenden Textabschnitten und die Bearbeitung der Aufgaben 1–5 erfolgt vorab im Rahmen einer Hausaufgabe, wobei nicht jede Schülerin/jeder Schüler alle fünf Aufgaben bearbeiten muss. Die Lehrkraft sollte vielmehr die Schülerinnen und Schüler des Kurses im Vorfeld in 5er-Schritten abzählen, sodass immer nur eine Aufgabe bearbeitet werden muss, jedoch auf die Gesamtsstärke des Kurses gesehen von verschiedenen Schülerinnen und Schülern arbeitsgleiche Aufgaben bearbeitet werden. Diese Schülerinnen und Schüler können dann zu Beginn einer Unterrichtsstunde Kleingruppen bilden, Ergebnisse ergänzen, auf den Punkt bringen und dem Kurs vortragen/präsentieren. Auf dieser Grundlage kann nachfolgend von der Lehrkraft ein Unterrichtsgespräch initiiert werden, dass sich an den Aufgaben 6 und 7 orientiert. Aufgabe 8 ist als schriftliche Aufgabe/Hausaufgabe einzusetzen.
In sehr leistungsschwachen Kursen ist von der Lehrkraft vor der Arbeit in Kleingruppen eine Sicherung des Textverständnisses einzuplanen.

Solutions

While reading tasks p. 18

Why make tea on a bunsen burner?

The Minister probably wants to demonstrate the low-tech, low impact of Ecotopian society (compared with elaborate kitchens in the US, for example).

What do the words 'compulsively' ... tell you about Weston's attitude to Ecotopia at this point?
They make it clear that Weston thinks all this 'fuss' about recycling is totally out of proportion. Why not carry on doing things in the American way as it then was?

While reading task p. 19

What are the implications of 'relatively sensible in scale'?
The Assistant Minister means that the kinds of reforms they believe in are easier to implement in a fairly small society. He is implicitly admitting that it would be hard to turn the whole of the US (let alone Russia, China or India) into an Ecotopia. In our world, too, it is generally agreed that it is easier to run small countries such as Denmark or Switzerland than larger countries such as Germany or the UK.

Activities p. 19

1. **Explain how a 'stable-state' basis for Ecotopian agriculture was achieved.**
   Points to make:
   - sewage recycling
   - garbage composting
   - animals not kept in close confinement

2. **Compare this system with the system in Germany.**
   Germany has a relatively good record on the recycling of household waste, filter systems for factories, etc. However, agriculture is generally on an industrial scale, and would not satisfy an Ecotopian, except for the production of organic ('Bio') products, which is a growth area, and would meet Ecotopian requirements. They would certainly be against experiments with genetically-modified plants, something which did not exist in Callenbach's day.

3. **Summarise the minister's views of the American 'disposal system'.**
   The minister uses the word 'dumped' to imply that sewage and industrial wastes of all kinds were 'disposed of', without much treatment to make them less toxic, in rivers, bays and oceans. (Landfill sites are not mentioned here, but the same criticisms apply.) The result of these practices, plus intensive farming, would be dead rivers and lakes. The minister goes on to say that the true costs of this apparently 'cheap' disposal system were being ignored in the rest of the US, but not, of course, in Ecotopia.

4. **Explain the difference between the terms 'disposal' and 'recycling'.**
   'Disposal' means to simply remove wastes from the place where they are produced and put them somewhere else. The effects these wastes may have on the environment are conveniently ignored until there is some kind of environmental disaster.
   'Recycling' means to treat as much waste material as possible in ways that make it possible for it to be re-used (e. g. organic fertilizers, glass, metals, plastic, paper).

Activities p. 20

5. **Why is the American 'disposal' system not as cheap as it seems?**
   Sooner or later the unpleasant effects of dumping waste away from the public eye will become obvious (fish dying, air pollution, contaminated earth, clusters of illnesses such as cancers), and it will then be much more expensive to remedy them than it would have been if good practices had been adopted from the outset. (Students should reminded that there are powerful environmental movements in modern America – *Ecotopia* was written more than 30 years ago.)

6. **We know that Weston decides to stay in Ecotopia at the end of his visit. In what areas do you think he will have to change his views?**
   Students can use their own general knowledge here as well as information from the text. The following attitudes would have to change:
   - waste disposal, farming, convenience foods and ways of cooking
   - waste creation

- personal transport – cars
- stable-state technologies
- importance of ecological criteria in all walks of life.

Note: (The fact that the resources of their vast country are not more or less infinite is one of the hardest lessons for Americans to learn. For a long time it seemed that way, and can be seen as a reason for what seem to us cavalier attitudes to energy consumption and the topics dealt with in Ecotopia. At the time of writing it would still be political suicide for an American president to raise tax on fuel to levels common in Europe.)

7. **The young men of Ecotopia take part in war games at regular intervals – and some of them actually get injured with spears. Why might Callenbach have felt it necessary to introduce this kind of activity?**
The most likely reason is that Callenbach will have felt that life in Ecotopia would be lacking in fun and excitement – it would all be rather low-key compared with the rest of America. Consequently, young men accustomed to driving around in hot rods, playing or watching very competitive sports etc. would need some kind of outlet for their energy. Hence the war games.

8. **On the basis of the information in the introduction and in the text, how would you feel about living in an Ecotopia-type world? Write a paragraph in which you discuss the pros and cons, and try to come to a conclusion.**
There is plenty of information in the SB for students to be able to argue the case from a personal point of view. Here are some useful expressions:
Well, of course I would like ...
I've always been interested in ...
I'm (not) the kind of person who ...
On the other hand ...
However ...
On balance ...
What I like about our world is ...
I'm not too happy about trends such as ...
If I had to make the choice, I ...
I think I would come down in favour of ...
What I really can't/couldn't stand is/would be (the way they/people) ...

Saving London

Juliette Jowit

About the photograph The photograph shows the barrier during construction or maintenance work. It normally retracts to the river bed so that shipping is not impeded, but it can be raised very quickly in case of emergency.

Unterrichtsempfehlungen

Es ist denkbar, die kleine Aufgabe unter „Before you read" im Vorfeld einer Schülerin/einem Schüler als Kurzreferat anzubieten. Im Unterricht kann der überschaubare Text nach dem Kurzreferat gelesen werden. Die Schülerinnen und Schüler sollten danach in einer Stillarbeitsphase die ersten drei Aufgaben („Holding back the floods") vorbereiten und sich diesbezüglich Notizen machen. In einem Unterrichtsgespräch werden die Aufgaben beantwortet; die Lernenden sollten dabei von der Lehrkraft daran erinnert wer-

den, einander zuzuhören, aufeinander zu reagieren und ggf. Beiträge von Mitschülerinnen und Mitschülern zu ergänzen oder auch richtigzustellen. In leistungsschwachen Kursen ist es ratsam, dass die Lehrkraft die wichtigsten Punkte während des Unterrichtsgespräches notiert und nach dem Unterricht als Ergebnissicherung den Schülerinnen und Schülern per E-Mail zukommen lässt. In sehr leistungsstarken Kursen mag diese Aufgabe auch von einem Schüler/einer Schülerin übernommen werden.
Während die Aufgaben 4 und 5 in kleinen Gruppen diskutiert bzw. bearbeitet werden und Ergebnisse im Anschluss unter den Gruppen ausgetauscht werden sollten, können die Aufgaben 6 und 7 als Hausaufgabe oder im Rahmen einer Stillarbeitsphase beantwortet werden. Aufgabe 7 kann in Form einer Tabelle/Gegenüberstellung (Text – Cartoon) stichpunktartig gelöst werden.

Solutions

Activities p. 21

1. **List global reasons why the Thames Barrier will sooner or later become out of date.**
   Points to make:
   - melting (land-based) ice causing rises in sea-levels
   - expanding sea water as temperatures rise

2. **Explain the 'Making Space for Water' strategy. How could it help to extend the life of the Thames Barrier?**
   This strategy aims to find large areas of (low-lying) land to which flood waters could be channelled during an emergency. The water would have to be channelled off downstream of the barrier, so that water levels at the barrier itself would not reach dangerous heights. If this strategy was successful, the barrier itself would not need to be raised or replaced for at least 50–80 years beyond 2030.

3. **What specific reasons are given for rising water levels in southern England (don't mention global warming in general).**
   Students should use their general knowledge as well as the information in the text.
   - Southern England is sinking at the rate of 1 mm. per year.
   - The London area is low-lying.
   - The Thames is a tidal river, so there is a threat from exceptionally high tides with the wind behind them.
   - The London area and the south-east generally are heavily built-up, which means that there are not very many open fields, etc. which could absorb some of the floodwater.

4. **Name some other areas which are likely to suffer from rising sea levels.**
   e.g. Bangladesh, Holland, various groups of islands, ...

5. **How would you characterise some of these areas?**
   low-lying, often subject to high tides, often densely-populated, often along river estuaries and deltas

6. **As you know, efforts to combat global warming seem unlikely to have very much effect. How should we try to deal with them – or can you think of ways in which we might after all avoid at least some of the consequences? Write a paragraph in which you express your personal views on the issues.**
   Points that could be made:
   - save energy at home
   - invest far more money in alternative sources of energy
   - protect low-lying areas
   - re-locate people living in the most highly-threatened areas

Personal views may range from optimistic – we can solve the problems if nations work together, to pessimistic – it's already too late, and China is still opening dozens of coal-fired power stations. What difference can smaller countries make, however clean and green they are?

7. **How can the cartoon below be related to the text about the Thames Barrier? Be careful – it's a catch question.**
Polar bears only live in the Arctic (around the North Pole), which consists entirely of ice, with no land underneath it. This means that the polar ice is already displacing its weight in water (Archimedes!), so its loss will not lead to a significant rise in sea levels (but expansion may play a role). This is good news for London, but no comfort for the polar bear in the cartoon!

Arctic Sea Ice Is Melting – Fast!

Steve Connor

About the photograph

Many photographs of this kind are appearing in the press. They document the fact that as a result of melting ice in areas inhabited by polar bears, life is becoming very difficult for them. Their habitat is gradually disappearing, and they may have to swim long distances from ice-floe to ice-floe in order to survive.

Unterrichtsempfehlungen

Der Einstieg könnte mithilfe des Fotos auf S. 22 in Verbindung mit der grafischen Darstellung („How Arctic ice is shrinking") S. 23 erfolgen. Möglicherweise ist es erforderlich, Vokabular bzw. Strategien zur Besprechung und Kommentierung von grafischen Darstellungen vorab zu wiederholen. Die Lektüre des Textes kann im Anschluss in Einzelarbeit erfolgen, die Sicherung des Textverständnisses anhand der Aufgaben 1–5 („Let's get this straight") geleistet werden, wobei Aufgabe 2 aufgrund des Einstiegs ausgespart werden sollte. Es ist denkbar, vor dem Hintergrund der Aufgabe 6 und 7 („The paradox") eine kontroverse Diskussion vorbereiten zu lassen, die von unterschiedlichen Interessengruppen bestritten wird (z. B. Umweltschutzgruppen wie Greenpeace oder Robin Wood – Interessengruppen aus der Öl- und Gas-Wirtschaft, die Nutzen aus den veränderten Bedingungen ziehen).
Alternativ dazu könnten in Kleingruppen kurze Reden vorbereitet werden, die das Plenum vom Standpunkt einer bestimmten Interessengruppe überzeugen sollen. Aufgabe des Plenums ist es, die überzeugendste Rede/den überzeugendsten Standpunkt begründend festzulegen, indem es sich darüber austauscht und Argumente abwägt.
Aufgabe 8 („Dramatic stuff") sollte schriftlich bearbeitet werden, z. B. im Rahmen einer Hausaufgabe oder Stillarbeitsphase.

Solutions

While reading task p. 23

Why is Denmark on this list?
Denmark has claims to parts of the Arctic via its links with Greenland.

Activities p. 23

1. **What is the general reason for the ice melting?**
Global warming

2. **Outline and comment on the information on the graph.**
We can assume that the graph was produced before the autumn of 2007 as the line

for that year is incomplete. The graph shows that the area covered by arctic ice used to decline during the summer and begin to recover by early autumn. In the past the area covered by ice was consistently higher than in the record year of 2005. In 2007 it looked as if this record would be broken, which would indicate a weak recovery in the autumn.

3. **Explain how the winter of 2007–2008 could be 'disappointing' (line 5).**
As ice formation in the previous winter was far below previous levels, and therefore 'disappointing', it seemed likely that the ability of the arctic to recover to anything like normal ice levels the following winter would also be disappointing. The graph for 2007 already shows a trend in this direction.

4. **Why does the exposure of more surface seawater lead to even faster melting of the ice?**
White ice reflects most of the solar energy, but dark seawater absorbs it and becomes warmer. This warmth is transferred to the ice.

5. **Comment on the fact that there is no mention of rising sea levels.**
The ice is floating on the sea and already displacing its weight.

6. **Explain in your own words the paradox referred to near the end of the article.**
The paradox is that as parts of the arctic seabed become accessible for the first time, oil and gas are likely to be extracted. Using this fuel will of course accelerate global warming, which was responsible for making these fuels available in the first place.

7. **What other groups might be pleased to discover less and less ice in the arctic?**
Shipping companies, explorers, researchers.

8. **Comment on the style of the article. Does it match up well with the subject matter? Where would you expect an article of this kind to appear?**
The article uses dramatic language for a topic which *is* potentially dramatic, e.g. 'shatter', 'really fast', 'an area seven times the size of England', 'rapid disintegration'. However, the general tone is serious, as befits a serious topic with global implications. We can assume that the writer is trying to 'wake readers up' to the seriousness of the situation, so some dramatic language is completely appropriate. This is the kind of article which one would expect to find in a broadsheet/serious newspaper, which is in fact the case.

Floating Houses

Elisabeth Kolbert

Unterrichtsempfehlungen

Auf der Grundlage einer gründlichen Lektüre des Textes können von den Schülerinnen und Schülern in Partnerarbeit die Aufgaben 1 und 2 beantwortet werden. Im Anschluss können die Antworten in einem kurzen Unterrichtsgespräch gesichert werden. Im Sinne einer Anwendungsorientierung ist es denkbar, die Aufgaben 1–3 für eine Präsentation in den Parallelkursen des Jahrgangs zu nutzen. Vor dem Hintergrund der Aufgaben 1 und 2 kann in Kleingruppen ein Vortrag erarbeitet werden, der z. B. durch eine Skizze auf einem Plakat oder einer Folie (*labelled drawing*) visualisierend unterstützt wird. Je nach technischer Ausstattung der Schule ist natürlich auch der Einsatz von Laptop und Beamer empfehlenswert. Nach dem Vortrag kann die Aufgabe 3 für eine Diskussion mit dem Parallelkurs herangezogen werden, wobei die Zuhörerschaft zu-

nächst eine Orientierungsphase erhalten sollte, um über tragfähige Möglichkeiten („Other solutions") nachdenken zu können.
Die Aufgabe 4 verlangt eine schriftliche Bearbeitung. Es ist zu empfehlen, die *essays* nach einer Endredaktion durch die Lehrkraft auf einer schulinternen e-learning Plattform abzustellen, sodass alle Schülerinnen und Schüler ihre *essays* austauschen und würdigen können. Vor dem Hintergrund dieses Austausches ist die Initiierung einer Diskussion (vgl. Aufgabe 5) denkbar.

Solutions

Activities p. 24

1. **Describe one of these floating houses for someone who has not seen the photos above.**
   Points to make:
   - look rather like toasters
   - moored to a metal pole
   - float on concrete pontoons
   - provide normal, quite spacious accommodation for a family
   - people living in them are very happy

2. **What problem are they designed to solve?**
   In low-lying areas, like much of Holland, there are a number of otherwise suitable housing sites which are subject to flooding on a regular basis. Floating houses make it possible to live in this kind of place. They are a very good solution in countries/ areas where population densities are high and other building land is not readily available.

3. **What other solutions can you think of to the problems of living on the water or in areas subject to flooding?**
   e.g. houseboats, living permanently on other kinds of boats, houses built on stilts, reclaiming low-lying land by building dykes and draining the land behind them

4. **Write a brief essay about the pros and cons of living in a floating house (novelty value? garden? getting ashore when the water rises? stormy weather?).**
   The points made above should help to get students started on their essay. They should be encouraged to use their imagination as well.
   Some further points to think about:
   - Would you need a little boat for times when the house is floating – and a jetty on higher land for getting out of it without getting your clothes muddy?
   - Would things fall off tables/furniture move around in a storm?
   - Could you be seasick in a *house*?
   - Would the house rock suddenly when boats go past as in the upper photograph?
   - What about the family car?

5. **Discuss your views with other students**
   Some useful expressions
   I really think it would be fun because ...
   I'm sure it would be very inconvenient in ways we haven't thought of ...
   You'd have to go and have a proper look round before buying one ...
   It doesn't say how expensive they are – I bet they cost a packet!
   I think I would be seasick – I'd be ill most of the time.
   I think a house should be firmly planted on dry land.
   How could Germans manage to live in a house without a proper cellar?
   (Houses of a similar type are being built on pontoons in some harbour areas in north Germany.)

The War against the Trees

Stanley Kunitz

About the poem

The poem is not particularly easy, but it has been included because it provides a very powerful description of the 'crime' of cutting down mature trees for commercial reasons. It is essential for students to hear the poem read out loud. It will work its magic even before they understand all the words.

About the author

Stanley Kunitz (1905–2006), an American born in Massachusetts, had a long and distinguished career as a poet. His work was influenced by the psychologist Jung, and he was awarded many honours during his long life, including the Pulitzer Prize, and a term as America's Poet Laureate. The English poet and novelist John Wain, who edited the anthology from which this poem was taken, claims that a poem by Kunitz, like a Shakespeare play, can be described as 'an extended metaphor'.

Unterrichtsempfehlungen

Die Schülerinnen und Schüler sollten sich gründlich mit dem Gedicht und dem Vokabular auseinandersetzen. Dies sollte im Rahmen einer Hausaufgabe vorab oder in einer Stillarbeitsphase erledigt werden.
Die Aufgaben 1–3 dienen der Sicherung des Textverständnisses und können in einem gelenktem Unterrichtsgespräch geleistet werden.
In einer Partnerarbeitsphase können die Aufgaben 4 und 5 bearbeitet und tabellarisch verschriftlicht werden. Nach dem Zufallsprinzip könnten einige Paare für eine Präsentationsphase mit Folie und Folienschreiber ausgestattet werden. Die Aufgaben 6 und 7 bieten sich hervorragend für ein Unterrichtsgespräch an. Dabei sollte die Lehrkraft darauf achten, dass die Schülerinnen und Schüler einander zuhören, aufeinander reagieren – kommunizieren!
Die abschließende Aufgabe („We're nearly all environmentalists now") ist schriftlich zu bearbeiten und dient dem Aufbau von Schreibroutine.

Solutions

Activities p. 26

1. **Explain what the poem is about in three or four sentences.**
   The action of the poem takes place on the day when a house-owner who has sold (part of) his garden to an oil company (so that they can build a filling station on it), joins his neighbours to watch the 'show' when the ancient elm trees in the garden are felled/cut down. The trees have already been trimmed, but before they come down, bulldozers have to undermine the roots. Finally they come down, leaving craters and huge tangled roots exposed to the view.

2. **Have a look at the first two lines. How does the tone differ from the rest of the poem?**
   In the first two lines the event is described as if it is harmless fun/a show, something the neighbours will want to come and watch/enjoy. In the rest of the poem felling the trees is seen as a crime/disaster/rape of nature/destruction of something irreplaceable.

3. **Now have a look at the last two lines. What new perspective do they add to the scene?**
   In the last two lines, the scene of devastation is distanced/made to seem less important/seen from the perspective of people driving past. They have another look at it in

their rear-view mirrors, but they are not really affected by it. They will probably shrug their shoulders, think it is a pity that the trees have gone, but then carry on with their lives as if nothing has happened.

4. **The poem is full of emotionally-charged words. Make a list of the most striking ones.**
   e.g. 'war', 'lopped and maimed', 'a northern seizure', 'forcing the giants to their knees', 'ghosts of children', 'death-foxed page', 'ripped', 'craters', 'bared their amputated coils', 'raw gorgons', 'pocks and scars'.

5. **How do these words tell you what the poet feels about the trees being cut down.**
   They link cutting down the trees with violent events/crimes/injuries of various kinds, such as war, rape, mutilation and amputation. The poet also feels that along with the environmental damage, history is being destroyed.

6. **Which parts of the poem convey the idea that a 'war' is being waged against the trees?**
   In particular lines 7–9 where specifically war-related terms are used ('foray', 'raid', 'war'), but of course the whole poem describes felling the trees as an attack.

7. **The fourth verse could be described as visionary. Why do you think the poet refers to the 'ghosts' of children?**
   As the trees fall, it is as if the poet sees the ghosts of children who once played in the shade of the trees racing out from under the branches to avoid being killed. As they come out into the sunlight we have to imagine a process rather like time-lapse photography. The ageing process is accelerated, and they end up as old people living out a miserable existence in the (treeless) suburbs.

8. **Choose an environmental issue or event which makes or has made you really angry. Try to write a really impassioned short article about it, using some emotive language to reinforce your case, as Kunitz has done.**
   Some additional vocabulary:
   sense of outrage, disgrace, environmental disaster, a tragedy for the community, must be prevented at all costs, will only benefit the developers, people were not properly consulted, everything was decided behind closed doors, will cause (noise) pollution, contamination, destroy an intact biosphere
   As this is intended to be an article, students should be reminded that they need to answer the usual 'wh- questions': who, when, where, why (not), as well as expressing their own opinions.

Worksheet 1

Fans of Old-Fashioned Lights Defy[1] a Government Phase-Out[2]

Elisabeth Rosenthal

On a quaint[3] lane called Camden Street, the sidewalk easel[4] stands out for its apocalyptic tone: “100-WATT BULBS IN STOCK. (FOR HOW LONG WE DO NOT KNOW).”

“Let some government official come in and tell me I can’t sell these,” Jonathan Wright, who has owned Classic Lighting for 40 years, said defiantly[5] as he surveyed his warren[6] of upscale[7] light fixtures and shelves filled with neatly stacked bulbs. “I’ll find them wherever I can get them and sell them for whatever they cost. People are buying in bulk because they want them.”

Mr. Wright says that in the last two months he has sold 3,000 of the 100-watt bulbs – the traditional mainstay[8] of British light fixtures – more than 30 times the usual. People are buying 10 at a time, the limit per customer, even though their price is nearly 50 percent higher than it was a year ago.

Mr. Wright’s store is on the front lines of resistance to controversial global efforts to end the era of energy-gobbling incandescent light bulbs[9] by phasing out their sale to encourage (or in Mr. Wright’s view, force) people to turn to more efficient compact fluorescents[10].

In Tunbridge Wells, the phase-out has brought howls of protest from people not normally prone to[11] rebellion. This is, after all, the quintessential well-heeled[12] English middle-class city – a place where Marks and Spencer[13] is the epicenter of a high street dotted with bookstores and cafes, where people still wear Wellington boots[14] and Conservatives win nearly every election.

Jenny Gale, 60, who said she had tried compact fluorescents while living in India, dislikes the new bulbs. “You can still find the old ones in stores that have some left, and for after that I’ll be stockpiling[15],” she said. “I’m not going to buy the new ones; I refuse. I hate the light.” Countries like Australia, Canada, the United States and the European Union nations have drafted varying plans to ban or restrict the sale of incandescent bulbs in the next few years. Sales of the bulbs will be banned in the European Union as of 2012, but Britain has moved especially swiftly: the government asked retailers to stop selling 75- and 100-watt bulbs as of Jan. 1. Most complied[16], including large chain stores, transforming the humble light bulb into a precious commodity[17].

---

1 **to defy** to resist
2 **phase-out** *stufenweiser Abbau*
3 **quaint** attractively old-fashioned
4 **easel** *here* wooden stand with an advertisement
5 **defiant** openly refusing sth.
6 **warren** *here* shop with many narrow passages
7 **upscale** adj., of a high quality and/or price
8 **mainstay** main object
9 **incandescent light bulb** *Glühlampe*
10 **compact flourescent** *Energiesparlampe*
11 **to be prone to** to be likely to do sth.
12 **well-heeled** infml., rich
13 **Marks and Spencer** British retailer mainly selling food and clothes
14 **Wellington boots** rubber boots
15 **to stockpile** to collect a large amount of goods
16 **to comply** to obey a command or rule
17 **commodity** a useful and valuable thing

Worksheet 1

Some consumers have calmly adapted to the green new world of compact fluorescents. "Seeing as that's the only ones we can buy now, I use them," said Katherine Allwood, a student. To get government credits for green initiatives, local electricity companies are even giving them out free of charge. But not everyone is taking.

"My mother tried them, and I said, 'Mother, my God, what have you done to your lights?'" said Pat Evans of South Godstone, northwest of here, who was out shopping. "For now, I have a good supply of normal bulbs, but I suppose they won't last forever."

Incandescent light bulbs used to have a clean image, representing the wonders of modern convenience (as in the phrase "as easy as changing a light bulb"). Yet in an age of global warming, the energy they consume – and waste – creates a public relations problem.

Lighting accounts for about 20 percent of global electricity use, or about 7 percent of global emissions. Incandescent bulbs, which dissipate the lion's share of their energy as useless heat, use 5 to 20 times more energy than the newer variants.

But the British have found themselves testing just how much people are willing to adjust long-held habits with the goal of greening the planet. (Like other European Union countries, Britain has promised to lower its emissions by 20 percent below 1990 levels by 2020.)

"Saving the planet is important, but it's not just about these bulbs," said Mr. Wright, the store owner. He said that compact fluorescent bulbs were fine for some fixtures that produced diffused lighting and that people should be educated to use them. (The bulbs can in theory screw into any fixture that takes an incandescent bulb.)

But their light is "awful" for many other lamps and fixtures, like reading lights and lighting near computers, since both types of compact fluorescents have a flicker, he said.

Indeed, his customers have a litany of complaints. The light is too dim, especially for reading and putting on makeup, they say; the bulbs, which are a bit longer than incandescents, protrude[18] from small light shades; they take a long time to reach full brightness; they cannot be dimmed by switches; they contain mercury[19] and therefore require special disposal.

Still, most stores here have abided by the government's request, if only to cultivate a green image. (Compliance is technically voluntary for now, since the European Union does not end incandescent sales until 2012.) At the local branch of Tesco's, Britain's largest supermarket chain, there are no 75- or 100-watt incandescents, and the array[20] of bulbs on display measures just 10 square feet or so. After all, if bulbs last six to 10 times as long, the display can be one-sixth the size. The compact fluorescent bulb considered equivalent to the 100-watt incandescent version sells for \$3.65; the old variant used to cost roughly \$1.

"People are switching because it's hard to buy normal bulbs now," said Mark Garnett, who works for an energy company. "They complain, but they do it."

---

[18] **to protrude** to stick out
[19] **mercury** *Quecksilber*
[20] **array** things placed in order

Worksheet 1

Many people say that the ban prompted them to do the right thing for the environment and that the inconvenience is minor. "I probably wouldn't have made the switch otherwise – only certain types of people would have done it voluntarily – so it's a good thing," said Scott Evans, a surveyor[21] here.

But for now, said Helen Nayak, 29, she and her husband are using compact fluorescents in their hallways only. They are saving "regular" bulbs for "rooms where we really want to see things," she said.

Elisabeth Rosenthal: "Fans of Old-Fashioned Lights Defy an Official Phase-Out", in: *New York Times*, www.nytimes.com, April 24, 2009 [Oct. 07, 2009]

---

[21] **surveyor** *Landvermesser*

Activities

1. **Draw simple sketches of the two kinds of bulbs referred to, with plenty of space round them. Now make notes on the arguments for and against each type round the two bulbs in the shape of stars. Compare results with a partner.**
2. **Bring in examples of the two types of bulb which, according to the information on them, or on the box, should provide an equal amount of light. Bring in two basic table lamps and the necessary calbes and sockets. Fit the bulbs to the lamps, plug them in fairly close to one another, in a darkened room if possible, and compare the quality/quantity of light and the (quoted) electricity consumption of the two bulbs. Make notes on your findings. Is it worth changing over?**
3. **Use the information you have collected above as the basis for an informal debate in which you take sides for or against energy-saving bulbs.**
4. **Fluorescent bulbs will probably turn out to be an interim solution. How else can we produce light from electricity? Time for a bit of research.**

Worksheet 1 Solution

1.

incandescent bulb	fluorescent bulb
for • cheap • does not stick out of light fittings • no dangerous chemicals used • not very high energy consumption compared with other domestic equipment	**for** • less energy consumed • highly efficient • also becoming cheap • very long life
against • short life • most of the energy used is turned into heat, not light • high energy consumption compared with energy-saving bulbs	**against** • most people don't like the tubular look • light quality felt by many people to be pale/ thin, too white, less bright than it should be according to the information provided (comparison with normal bulb wattage) • dangerous chemicals used, which will need to be treated as toxic waste • the bulbs stick out of some light fittings • there is some flickering • take some time to reach full brightness

2. Free activity

3.
Some useful expressions:
- We've tried energy-saving bulbs, but no one likes them!
- I don't really care if the old bulbs use a bit more electricity – they're much nicer!
- How do you mean, 'nicer'?
- Well, they look nicer, and the light is warmer, more natural somehow.
- The flickering would really get on my nerves.
- They're OK down in the cellar – but not in the living room.
- They just don't light up a room properly – there's something wrong with the quality of the light.
- Let's face it – energy-saving bulbs are ugly.
- But they save money.
- How much money – I bet it's only a couple of Euros per year!

4.
Students will be able to find out that **LED** (light-emitting-diode) lightning will propably be the long-term solution. They are very compact, energy efficient and have a very long life. There are some problems with achieving the right colouring for the light output, but they can be solved.
Halogen bulbs have been in use for decades, particulary for spots and in car headlights. Most people are happy with the colour of the light, they also have quite a long life, but they are not much more economical than incandescent bulbs.
Neon tubes (display lightning) and **Xenon equipment** (expensive, very bright car head-lights) are mentioned in the interests of completeness. **Carbon arc lights** – extremely bright lights used in old cinema projectors – are not suitable for use in the home!

Air and Energy

Producing Energy

Unterrichtsempfehlungen

Die *picture gallery* eignet sich nicht nur hervorragend als Hinführung zum übergeordneten Thema „Air and Energy", sondern auch zum Aufbau von Vokabular und *phrases*, um über die verschiedenen Formen der Energiegewinnung mit ihren Vor- und Nachteilen in der Zielsprache sprechen bzw. diskutieren zu können. Abhängig von den in einem Kursquartal tatsächlich zur Verfügung stehenden Unterrichtsstunden, ist es zu empfehlen, dass sich die Lehrkraft eine Unterrichtseinheit Zeit nimmt, um gemeinsam mit den Schülerinnen und Schülern *mind maps* und *phrase banks* zu erstellen bzw. aufzubauen. Diese sollten dann im Sinne einer *rich learning environment* in Form von Postern an den Wänden den Schülerinnen und Schülern Hilfestellung bei der Sprachproduktion leisten.

Solutions

Before you read p. 27

The drawings in the 'picture gallery' below show some of the main ways in which we produce energy. Name them and say something about their effect on the environment (if any).

1.	Nuclear power station	No emissions of greenhouse gases, but possible contamination of surroundings, and major disposal problems for nuclear waste.
2.	Open-cast mining	Major earth-moving, re-settling and destruction of landscape (but land is often reclaimed and turned into a new landscape with lakes etc.). The coal mined is usually brown coal/lignite, which is a 'dirty' fuel.
3.	Solar energy (panels)	Totally emission-free production of electricity, but good supplies of sunlight are essential (there are also panels which produce hot water).
4.	Oil or gas platform	Pumps up oil or gas from below the sea bed. Familiar pollution/global warming problems when the fuel is burnt.
5.	Wind generators/ wind farm	Totally emission-free production of electricity, but relies on wind. Some noise pollution near rotors. Maintentance expenses may reduce the ratio of benefits to costs.
6.	Geo-thermal power station	Energy from below the earth's surface is used. An excellent option in areas with high levels of volcanic activity.
7.	Dam – hydro-electric power	Another source of clean electricity, but dambuilding can be environmentally questionable (see SB p. 13–14).
8.	Production of methane from bio-waste	A good way of producing energy from waste products, not at present practised on a large scale.

CCS Carbon Capture and Storage: There are plans to pump CO_2 into disused mines/ natural cave systems/empty gas and oil reservoirs under the seabed.

Conventional or Alternative?

About the photograph

The photograph shows a single wind generator next to a conventional power station, billowing clouds of steam (condensation) from its cooling towers and, by implication, pollutants from its chimneys which are not in view.

Unterrichtsempfehlungen

Die unterrichtliche Auseinandersetzung folgt dem Frageimpuls *Which side are you on, ...* (S. 28 oben). Allerdings sollte die Lerngruppe zunächst nur das Foto (entweder mithilfe einer Folie oder Laptop/Beamer) wahrnehmen, zu Spontanäußerungen und folgend zu einer genauen Beschreibung angeregt werden.

Solution

Text and photo p. 28

Supporters of conventional or alternative forms of power could each use the photograph below to support their cases. Which side are you on, and how would you support your case, using the photograph as a starting point for an informal debate?

Points which could be made:
- far more power from the conventional power station
- reliable power from the power station
- high levels of pollution
- Wind generator will only operate intermittently.
- relatively small output unless part of a wind farm
- Large tracts of countryside/coastal sea areas would have to be covered with wind generators to create a really significant amount of wind power.
- However, the electricity produced in this way is emission-free.
- We would always need some conventional or nuclear power stations for backup on days with no wind.
- Maintenance costs for wind generators are a significant factor affecting their overall efficiency.

Some useful expressions:
- Of course I'm in favour of clean energy/wind power, but ...
- I wouldn't want to live underneath a wind generator/next door to a power station.
- Nuclear power is the only real answer.
- Oh no, it isn't! What about these clusters of cancers we read about?
- There's no evidence that they have anything to do with the power station.
- If you believe that, you'll believe anything.
- They'll get this CCS working sooner or later.
- By then the Chinese coal-fired power stations will have wrecked the planet!
- The Chinese are already building a cleaner generation of coal-fired power stations.
- The only long-term solution is solar power – we just have to put the solar power stations in places with plenty of sun.
- In my view, we'll always need a mix of different power sources – more clean energy as time goes on. We're a clever species. We can crack the problems.
- By then London and Holland will be under water!

Cars, Cars, Cars

Stephen Speight

About the text

This text by the editor is an attempt to look at 'der Deutschen liebstes Kind' in the context of energy shortages and worries about pollution and global warming. At the time of writing, the German car industry was making belated efforts to produce economical cars, but their worldwide reputation, and their sales, particularly in rich and emerging countries, depend on sales of fairly large, high-quality vehicles. These are never going to be really economical, even in hybrid form.

About the photographs

Photograph of major road/motorway in China
The sun appears to be shining, but as a result of smog the daylight has a peculiar semi-transparent quality. Vehicles disappear into the smog about a kilometre away from the viewpoint.
SUV
This Hyundai SUV was included as a typical example of the species. It is quite clearly designed to impress – even intimidate – other road users. At the time of writing, large SUVs and 4 x 4s were generally unpopular as the result of energy and economic crises. A second-hand version of a car such as a Range Rover or a Porsche Cayenne which will have cost around € 80,000 when new, could be bought for around € 25,000 a couple of years later.
Greenpeace protest
This car has been fitted with a pig's snout to demonstrate Greenpeace's views of thirsty German cars. Whether or not this protest was fair is something students could discuss. VW is no worse than most other manufacturers and better than some, although, if this was a VW Touareg (a large 4 x 4), then a protest would probably have been justified. Another point: is it right for Greenpeace to try and damage the German car industry in this way?

Background information

A hybrid car uses an electric motor to drive the car, usually for short distances only/in town and sometimes to boost acceleration. Its advantages are to some extent counterbalanced by the need to carry heavy batteries. Fully electric cars are beginning to be produced, but in most, if not all, cases, these cars are too expensive to be of interest to normal buyers. They are beginning to appear in cities, etc., subsidised or bought outright by local councils. Fuel cell cars (which produce energy from hydrogen, and only water as exhaust) are another high-tech, high cost option, used in buses in some places. Again expense, and how to produce hydrogen in large quantities without creating pollution, are major problems.

Unterrichtsempfehlungen

Die Arbeit mit dem Text und den Aufgabenapparat bietet zwei Möglichkeiten. Die Lektüre des Textes erfolgt zu Hause. Die Aufgaben zu „Des Deutschen liebstes Kind" und „Let's get technical" werden auf zwei Gruppen verteilt und jeweils zu Hause vorbereitet. In einer Unterrichtseinheit werten die Schülerinnen und Schüler ihre Ergebnisse dann aus und führen sie zusammen. Beide Gruppen sollten dann in einem weiteren Schritt eine Präsentation vorbereiten, die nicht nur die Fragen sukzessiv abarbeitet, sondern kreativ die Oberthemen „Des Deutschen liebstes Kind" bzw. „Let's get technical" zusammenhängend berücksichtigt. Hier sind inszenierte Dialoge, Interviews, szenisches Spiel ebenso denkbar wie Kurzvorträge mithilfe von Plakaten und Folien.
Eine weitere Möglichkeit ist es, den gesamten Aufgabenapparat für ein Stationenlernen zu nutzen:

Station 1: Des Deutschen liebstes Kind
Station 2: Let's get technical
Station 3: You and your car
Station 4: Personal transport – the future
Hier ist die Lehrkraft jedoch im Vorfeld über das übliche Maß der Unterrichtsvorbereitung gefordert, da sie für die Bearbeitung einiger Fragen Zusatztexte und Zusatzmaterial suchen und bereitstellen muss.
Da sich in sehr vielen Fachschaften mittlerweile Teamarbeit und ein intensiver Austausch unter den Kolleginnen und Kollegen durchgesetzt hat, ist besonders bei der Entscheidung für das Stationenlernen in diesem Fall eine enge Zusammenarbeit mit Kolleginnen und Kollegen der Parallelkurse empfehlenswert.

Solutions

Activities p. 30

1. Collect some statements from your class about the quality and image of German cars.

Original student contributions, but here are some suggestions:
- We make the world's best cars.
- We've got a Mercedes/BMW/Audi, and it's a fantastic car.
- Those are cars for yuppies/snobs/rich people/managers.
- Rubbish, you're just jealous. What have you got at home – a Fiat?
- No, it's a Skoda – don't laugh, they're made by VW, and they're just as good or better – and a bit cheaper.
- German cars are too expensive anyway.
- That's because they're better made.
- Yours may be – we've had a lot of trouble with ours – for example it broke down/we've had some expensive repairs to the engine/gearbox, we've had trouble with the electrics/the electronics
- But most of them are too thirsty – ours too.
- I'm not interested in cars – I go everywhere by bike or public transport, so my conscience is clear, and I don't know what all the fuss is about.
- I really hate Porsche drivers, and drivers of big SUVs.
- Envy is a nasty emotion!

2. Do the same for foreign cars (sort the statements according to the other main car-manufacturing countries) .

Prejudices are bound to come into play here. Teachers should allow students to voice them, but try to counterbalance them where necessary.

France
- good little cars
- carelessly built
- liable to rust
- economical
- comfortable
- no really successful premium models
- some models (vans etc.) extremely practical

Italy
- some fantastic high-performance cars (Ferrari, Maserati)
- something special about Alfa Romeos – but not always very reliable
- Fiats are generally good little cars with some reliability problems.

- economical, generally cheap to run
- some models very practical

Japan
- Most Japanese cars are very reliable and well-made.
- no real price advantage compared with European cars
- Some models still lack individuality.
- pioneers of hybrid cars
- Toyota has taken over from General Motors as the world's largest motor manufacturer.

The US
- relied for far too long on the production of cheap, thirsty pickups and SUV's
- has never taken economy or high-tech engineering seriously
- now paying the price
- But long ago huge American cars, as seen in old Hollywood films, were the envy of the world. Still impressive when you see restored models over here, but they look out of place in the modern world – have become dinosaurs.

Britain
- no British-owned major manufacturer (Rolls Royce and Bentley are German-owned – and don't make many cars anyway)
- reputation of British cars ruined in the now fairly distant past
- Jaguar and Land Rover still famous names – factories Indian-owned, future uncertain
- A number of Japanese factories produce cars in Britain.

3. **Discuss the future of the German car industry on this basis, taking into account the increasing impact of high fuel prices and environmental issues.**
   Points which could be made:
   - excellent engineering skills available
   - Germany can make very good small cars, but the competition from abroad is tough.
   - The premium image of German manufacturers must be maintained at all costs. As pointed out in the text, it's Germany's USP (unique selling proposition).
   - German manufacturers need to react faster to new trends/demands.
   - Their cars have some reliability problems, but these are being addressed.
   - Economy plus premium quality plus innovation should be the watchwords.

4. **Germany is proud of its record on recycling and other environmental issues, but there is no general speed limit on the *Autobahn*. Write a short speech for or against such a speed limit, and use it in an informal debate on the issue.**
   Points for a speed limit:
   - less (serious/fatal) accidents
   - lower fuel consumption
   - less air pollution
   - less noise pollution

   Points against a speed limit:
   - A speed limit may adversely affect sales of German cars – they will no longer be '*Autobahn*-tested'.
   - High-performance cars would lose their *raison d'être*.
   - Drivers may lose concentration – driving will be more boring.
   - Some evidence that a speed limit causes bunching and increased shunt-type accidents (*Auffahrunfälle*).

5. **What is the problem with CO_2? After all, it's just the stuff which makes fizzy drinks fizzy, isn't it?**
Carbon dioxide is not at all poisonous, but it is an effective greenhouse gas – i. e. it reflects the sun's rays back down to earth – just as the glass in a greenhouse traps some of the sun's energy

6. **How does a hybrid car work?**
There are various types. A generator driven by the car's conventional engine is used to charge batteries, which can then power an electric motor. This electric motor can drive the car (usually for short distances), or boost acceleration. There is a gain in economy and reduction in pollution because a hybrid car can travel some distance in town on the electric motor alone. The extra weight of the two 'engines' and the batteries is a weakness of the concept.

7. **Could electric cars be the answer?**
A tricky question. At present conventional liquid fuels contain about twenty times the energy of a battery of the same weight. But batteries will become gradually more efficient, so the range of electric cars will increase. There is no infrastructure to charge or replace batteries at present, but this may be in the pipeline. It will also be possible to plug in an electric car at home. If electric cars become widespread, electricity consumption (much of it from conventional power stations), will increase significantly, and along with it pollution, but not in city streets.

8. **To what extent are diesel engines better for the environment than petrol engines?**
Diesel engines are generally more economical than petrol engines of the same size, and function at lower engine speeds, so the actual quantity of exhaust gases is smaller. However, while a conventional catalytic converter cleans up petrol exhausts effectively, even a particle filter for diesels does not clean up the exhaust completely. Some new cars remove these pollutants, but only in models at the top of the range at present. Two further points: petrol engines are becoming more efficient all the time – the economy gap is closing, and diesel fuel contains slightly less energy than petrol, so the apparent advantage is not as large as it seems.

9. **What role does driving style play in saving fuel?**
A very large role. A light foot on the accelerator, plus intelligent anticipation to avoid sudden braking, plus keeping the revs down in the gears, plus moderate cruising speeds can improve consumption figures dramatically.

10. **What kind of car would you like one day? Or would you rather own no car at all? Or a motor cycle? If you like, you can choose a dream car and a more practical car. Explain your choice(s) to your fellow-students.**
This activity can safely be left to students. If there is time, students could produce short presentations backed up with photographs/drawings etc.

11. **What do you think cars will be like half a century from now? Or won't there be any?**
Personal views. Some of the options:
   - very small, economical cars otherwise similar to today's cars
   - electric or fuel cell cars
   - systems to link and control cars on the motorways
   - gradual disappearance of personal transport as fossil fuels run out
   - new sources of fossil fuel will enable us to carry on much as before
   - as so many people love their cars, some form of personal transport will almost certainly survive (essential in country areas where there are hardly any buses)

12. What is the message of the cartoon on the previous page?
A report on world climate in the form of a giant book is blocking the road. An SUV or 4 x 4 sees the obstacle ahead and simply goes off-road (another name for this kind of vehicle) to avoid it. The message is that the kind of people who drive this kind of car don't care what their vehicles are doing to the climate and will not support legislation to improve the environment (higher fuel taxes which would hit them hard, for example).
(Punitive congestion charges to keep this kind of vehicle out of Central London caused outrage among owners of vehicles covered by the charge, which would include motor homes as well as SUVs, 4 x 4s and some vans.)

13. The photo below shows the world's cheapest car, the Tata Nano, which its Indian makers hope will mobilise their vast nation. Find out more about this car, and try to assess its potential, good or bad.
Google had over 8 million entries for the Nano at the time of writing, including Wikipedia, and car magazines cover its development and progress at fairly regular intervals, so there is no shortage of information.
The potential for putting Indian families on the road is enormous, but so is the pollution danger, with a market eventually of hundreds of millions of cars. The version for the Indian market has no catalytic converter and little or no safety gear. Models for the European market, if it is ever imported, will be better equipped.

A Car-lover's Lament

Chris Chilton

Unterrichtsempfehlungen

Die Lektüre des Artikels kann im Unterricht vorgenommen werden. Vielleicht ist die einfache Erstellung eines Hörtextes denkbar, indem die Lehrkraft einen befreundeten *native speaker* (z. B. eine Kollegin/ein Kollege einer Partnerschule der Zielkultur) darum bittet, den Text zu sprechen und zu digitalisieren. Ein simpler Austausch der Daten (Text – Hörtext in return) per E-Mail hat sich diesbezüglich bewährt und stellt keinen großen Aufwand dar. Eine vertiefende Sicherung des Textverständnisses kann mithilfe der ersten drei Fragen vorgenommen werden. Die Bearbeitung der Aufgaben 4 und 5 erfordert eine vorbereitende Recherche und sollte beispielsweise im Rahmen einer Hausaufgabe von den Schülerinnen und Schülern erledigt werden. Alternativ ist ein lebendiger, adressatengerechter Lehrervortrag möglich, der die Impulse aus den Aufgaben 4 und 5 aufgreift. Die Aufgaben 7 und 8 verlangen eine Bearbeitung in schriftlicher Form. Es ist denkbar, die Schülerinnen und Schüler eine der beiden Aufgaben auswählen zu lassen.

Solutions

1. Explain in two or three sentences what worries the author about the trend towards more environmentally-acceptable cars. Activities p. 32
He accepts that cars will have to become safer, quieter and greener in the future, but he is worried that at some point the fun element will get lost.
Everyone may end up driving low-powered cars running on thin tyres, and this will not be an enjoyable driving experience. Perhaps, as a protest against this situation, some 'car-mad loonies' may end up racing around the country in thirsty old bangers.

2. **What does he mean by a 'tipping point'?**
   A point at which there is a sudden change in a process, possibly also a point of no return. In the case of cars, it would mean the point where all the additional safety and environmental equipment begins to outweigh the advantages of modern technology, so that cars (which he believes have improved continually until now) become gradually less good (in his terms) from this point on.

3. **What two options does he see for himself in the future?**
   He could either turn into a rebel driving a fast, noisy, old car, or 'drive' a futuristic model which joins a motorway car train (see answer 6 below) to London so that he can read a digital newspaper as he goes along.

4. **Explain how thin tyres and high gearing can save petrol/diesel.**
   Thin tyres have less rolling resistance/friction in contact with the road because less area touches the road surface.
   High gearing means that the engine turns more slowly for a given road speed, which again reduces friction within the engine and saves fuel. However, if the gearing is too high, the car feels 'unwilling', because the engine is not turning fast enough to produce an acceptable amount of power, and it may be necessary to use larger throttle openings or change down in order to improve performance – which would cancel out the advantages of the high gearing.

5. **If you don't already know about these things, find out what common devices for cleaning up exhaust gases are already fitted to nearly all modern cars, and explain how they work.**
   The main devices are **catalytic converters** for petrol engines, which convert most of the toxic gases into harmless substances such as water. A catalyst (platinum) is used to speed up/facilitate this process, but the catalyst is not itself affected by the exhaust gases.
   For diesel engines **particle filters** are a partial answer to dirty exhausts. The filter absorbs nearly all the soot particles in diesel exhausts, which are believed to be carcinogenic. More advanced systems which deal with other pollutants are on the way.

6. **What might a 'motorway car train' be?**
   A motorway car train would be a convoy of cars travelling down a motorway, with electronic equipment regulating speed and steering. There would be no need for the drivers to do anything, and as the cars would be very close together, there would be savings in fuel consumption because the 'train' would be more streamlined than the same number of cars travelling separately. In some experiments, cars are guided by a cable under the road surface.

7. **What features of this article show that it was written by a good motoring journalist for an up-market car magazine?**
   e.g.
   - He knows all the terms for different car-types (coupé-cabriolet, crossover ...).
   - He uses 'insider' terms for car parts, e.g. rubber for tyres, cogs for gears.
   - He assumes a knowledgeable readership – these terms are not explained nor are Blue motion (super-clean and economical VW technology) or the 2CV, which Germans call *hässliches Entlein*.
   - He speaks in a familiar way to fellow-enthusiasts, e.g. 'the hardcore enthusiasts among you'.
   - The style is generally interesting for car-lovers to read, e.g. '... the pleasure derived from future cars will all be related to the quality of the leather covering the car-to-car interface ...'

8. What is your attitude to cars and driving? Fun, convenience, or something we should learn to do without altogether? Write a paragraph expressing your views, and discuss them with your fellow-students.

Personal views, with plenty of useful information given in the previous texts in this unit. Some useful expressions:
I'm sure I will really enjoy driving/learning to drive.
It's part of the growing up process.
It's a dangerous business for young drivers.
Being behind the wheel is a great feeling!
I'm not really interested in driving – I'd rather be driven or use public transport.
I'm (seriously) worried about the environmental impact of cars.
Cars aren't half as bad as lorries/trucks, planes, power stations ...
You just can't beat the family car for convenience/major shopping trips/getting furniture home from IKEA/camping holidays ...
As long as cars go on becoming more economical, I don't see a problem.
I'm a car freak – I can't imagine life without a car.

The Price of Oil

Text and graph

It was felt to be advisable to include a German text in the SB, because students will often find themselves working with their first language and English in the world of work. In this case the text and graph outline some of the 'mileposts' in the development of oil prices from 1957 to 2007. At the time of writing (during the 2008–9 recession) there was a dramatic fall in oil prices as production slowed down worldwide. However, the long-term trend is bound to be upwards as fossil reserves begin to run out and consumption resumes its inexorable rise.

Unterrichtsempfehlungen

Rasanter Anstieg

Die Bedeutung von Sprachmittlung nimmt vor dem Hintergrund von Migration, Globalisierung und Europäisierung eine bedeutende Stellung ein. Die interlinguale Kommunikation von Inhalten aus einer Sprache in die andere ist fast schon ein Normalfall der Alltagskommunikation in unserer und anderen Gesellschaften geworden. Sowohl der Gemeinsame Europäische Referenzrahmen als auch die KMK legen deshalb ausdrücklich das Kompetenzziel Sprachmittlung fest.
Abhängig von der Vertrautheit des Kurses mit Techniken der Sprachmittlung, können der deutsche Text mit der grafischen Darstellung und die *Activity* zunächst in einer Stillarbeitsphase oder Hausaufgabe gründlich vorbereitet werden. Die sprachmittelnde Person muss dabei auf die Überprüfung des Mediationsprozesses achten (u. a. Hat mein Zuhörer alles verstanden?); die Zuhörerin/der Zuhörer sollte angehalten werden, bei Bedarf Rückfragen zu stellen. Einige nach dem Zufallsprinzip ausgewählte Partner sollten im Anschluss ihre Mediation vor dem gesamten Kurs vorstellen, im Plenum auswerten und würdigen lassen. Im Fall, dass ein Kurs nur wenig mit Mediationsprozessen vertraut ist, sollte vorab in einem anschaulichen Lehrervortrag der Sinn von Sprachmittlung, Strategien der Sprachmittlung auf den Punkt gebracht werden – den Schülerinnen und Schülern sollte auf jeden Fall klar sein, dass hier die wörtliche Übersetzung nicht das Ziel ist.

change course and start producing economical vehicles in time, serves as a lesson to other car companies and other countries. Whether countries such as China and India, with growing economies and energy needs, will see reducing emissions as their responsibility is another matter. These countries like to point out that, per person, their emissions are still much lower than those in the old industrial countries, but there are nevertheless signs that they are beginning to take their environmental responsibilities seriously.

5. The film referred to on p. 35 is a 'disaster movie'. What features would you expect to find in a film of this type?

Some typical features:

- lots of action
- tough hero gets/saves the girl
- very impressive special effects of various kinds
- bad guys don't survive
- the planet/city/country is saved at the last minute
- characters tend to be stereotypes, not very complex

Activities p. 37

6. Explain the term 'peak oil'. Why is this an important concept for our world?

Peak oil is the point in time at which the highest world output of oil is reached. From this point on oil output will slowly decline, while consumption is likely to go on increasing until there is a crash of some kind. Peak oil is an important concept because it reminds us that oil supplies are finite, which means that if we don't reduce consumption in the short term and find alternatives in the longer term, our world is heading for disaster.

7. What is the film's message?

The message is simple enough. If we don't start reducing consumption immediately, all kinds of disasters are imminent. (Presumably the film-makers did not realise that a world-wide recession of the kind which occurred in 2008 – 9 would considerably reduce oil consumption and oil prices.)

8. Why is Loughhead less worried about dwindling oil supplies from conventional sources than the makers of *A Crude Awakening*?

- He points out that expensive oil makes it economic for oil companies to exploit less accessible oil fields.
- Melting ice means that some of these fields will not be too difficult and expensive to exploit anyway.
- Coal and gas can easily be turned into liquid fuel.
- We could speculate whether Loughhead is to some extent under the influence of the oil companies.

9. Environmentalists would be worried by some of Loughhead's statements. Which statements, and why?

E. g. 'There are many other types of fuel that we could exploit.' (ll. 23/24)

This is a worrying statement because it completely ignores the need to use less fuel generally in order to reduce emissions. It also ignores the consequences of using large areas of farming land to grow crops which can be turned into fuel.

'... many, many more reserves suddenly become economical – the oil tar fields of Alaska, deep water reservoirs, and others' (ll. 29 – 31)

Here it is the horrendous environmental consequences of exploiting some of these sources of oil which Loughhead ignores.

10. Do you think we will 'run out of oil' (or have to pay really astronomical prices for it) in the fairly near future? Make some notes on your views and discuss them in class.

Points which could be made:

- Although oil stocks are finite, there are still enormous quantities available.
- But consumption is also rising all the time (with short-term drops in consumption due to economic factors).
- It is hard to imagine a long-term reduction in oil consumption.
- Electric cars are on the way, but fuel for them is simply burnt at power stations instead of in the car itself (whether electric cars are actually more economical than conventional cars if all factors are taken into account is a disputed point).
- It will be a long time before there are affordable electric cars on the market.
- If we can learn to harness solar energy efficiently, we will have all the power we need. A small patch of the Sahara would meet all Germany's energy needs – the technology is available, but the logistical and political problems are enormous.

Why We Must Give up Flying

Nicholas Crane

About the cartoon

The cartoon shows a giant arm coming down from a cloud. The rather nice embroidered cuff on the sleeve shows that this is God's arm. He is holding a crook or crozier, one of the symbols of office of bishops and other senior church dignitaries. God is using his crook to pull an airliner out of the sky.
This God clearly shares the views of the God who wrote to George W. Bush on p. 36.

Unterrichtsempfehlungen

Für die Arbeit mit dem Text und den *Activities* empfiehlt sich eine vorbereitende Hausaufgabe. Die Schülerinnen und Schüler sollten den Auftrag erhalten, den Text gründlich zu lesen und stichpunktartig die Fragen 1 – 7 (*One man's views* und *A voice crying in the wilderness*) zu beantworten.
Im Unterricht kann dann eine Gruppenarbeitsphase stattfinden, in der die Gruppen ein Interview mit Crane entwickeln. Dafür können die Fragen 1 – 7 umformuliert und auch zusätzliche Interviewfragen eingebracht werden. Das Interview kann dann inszeniert und dem Plenum vorgestellt werden. Dabei sind der Kreativität fast keine Grenzen zu setzen, die Schülerinnen und Schüler sollten motiviert werden, ein packendes, interessantes Interview sowie Geschehen um das Interview herum in Szene zu setzen. Die Lehrkraft sollte in Erwägung ziehen, einige Interviews, u.a. auch für eine Fokussierung der sprachlichen Leistung, zu videografieren. Die Aufgabe 8 kann für eine abschließende Diskussion im Plenum herangezogen werde. Aufgabe 9 kann hingegen als Hausaufgabe erledigt werden, wobei jeweils 2 Partner ihre Fragen bzw. Antworten per E-Mail austauschen. In ausgedruckter Form könnten Fragen und Antworten an eine Pinwand im Kursraum geheftet werden.

Solutions

Before you read p. 37

Ten years ago (Nicholas Crane) decided never to fly again. An extreme view, of course, in an age of cheap flights for ordinary people. What do you think?

Points which could be made:

- There probably should be less cheap flights – people go to places they don't really need to see and would never have dreamed of visiting in the past.
- If there were no more cheap flights, flying would become something only rich people could afford – as in the fairly recent past. This would be a bad thing – a new form of elitism.
- It's all very well for Crane to give up flying – he's already flown all over the world.
- I personally do/do not want to go on cheap flights because I think I have the same rights as everyone else/because I worry about the environmental impact.

Activities p. 39

1. Summarise Crane's pre-1998 view of the environment.
He knew about the dangers, but as a travel writer he saw no reason not to fly to distant parts of the world, often for just a short visit. He wrote about the places he visited with enthusiasm and may well have persuaded a lot of other people to fly to these destinations.
When he got to his destination he travelled by bicycle or on foot, but savings over these relatively short distances (compared with non human-powered transport) will have been insignificant.

2. What caused him to change his mind?
He attended a lecture on the hole in the ozone layer, and not long afterwards he became aware of global warming. Until then he had assumed that the atmosphere was capable of dealing with pollutants. Now he realised that mankind was facing as great a threat as the last Ice Age.

3. Explain why he feels personally responsible for global warming to some extent.
Two points can be made:
- He flew all over the world as a travel writer, certainly 'clocking up' more air miles than an average person.
- His enthusiasm for the places he visited may have led to large numbers of people flying to these destinations who would not have thought of going there until they read Crane's articles or saw his TV programmes.

4. How has his life as a travel writer changed since he gave up flying?
He now only travels to places that can be reached by train, so he is more or less limited to Britain and mainland Europe. However, he has found that he can continue to earn his living as a travel writer on 'home ground'. There are plenty of wonderful/undiscovered places in Britain and the rest of Europe which he can draw people's attention to.

5. Explain what Crane means by 'non-adapters' to climate change.
He is referring to educated people who know the facts about climate change, but simply decide to ignore them and continue living the same kind of 'high-energy' life as before (driving thirsty cars, frequent flights, etc.).

6. List the points which 'non-adapters' make in order to defend their views.
They claim:
- that there is no connection between human activity and climate change
- that climate change is good for cold parts of the planet like Clydeside
- that aircraft emissions actually counteract global warming by adding a 'heat-shield' of pollutants to the atmosphere (a scientifically untenable argument).

7. Why doesn't he agree with them?
Because he has himself undergone a 'conversion' to a low-energy life-style, and cannot understand why other people are not equally worried about the environmental consequences of carrying on as before.

8. "Why shouldn't the next generation have the same fun?" Crane can't answer this question. As members of the 'next generation' what would your answers be?
Possible answers:
- We have the same rights that Crane had when he was younger – let's fly!
- He's making a serious point. The modern debate about global warming had not started then, whereas we know about the dangers, so perhaps we don't have the same right to go on cheap flights.
- Whether or not young people go on cheap flights won't really make any difference. The flights will take off anyway, so we may as well be on board.
- If large numbers of young people set an example by refusing to fly, they could actually help to reduce the number of cheap flights, which would be a good thing for the environment.

9. Re-formulate Crane's final question for someone living in Germany, and put it to your fellow-students.
E. g. 'Why go to New Zealand if you haven't seen the sun set over the Alps, the North Sea or the midnight sun in Norway and Sweden?'
Individual answers, some students will probably be happy to see the setting sun/ spend holidays in areas they can get to by car, train or ship, others will want to go further afield.
The supporters of European destinations can say there are just as many beautiful places here as anywhere else on earth, and give examples. The 'birds of passage' can point out that Europe is all a bit too familiar/civilised/not exotic enough.
People suffering from *Wanderlust* will point out that there are scenes out there (the Painted Desert, Greenland, Pacific Islands, India, the Himalayas ...) which simply have no equivalents here 'at home'.

The Last Century for Man

Marillion

Unterrichtsempfehlungen

Die Lehrkraft sollte sich um eine Aufnahme des Songs bemühen. Sie sollte den Schülerinnen und Schülern die Informationen, die im Einleitungstext auf S. 39 zu finden sind, mitteilen, dabei halten die Lernenden ihre Bücher geschlossen. Die Schülerinnen und Schüler hören dann den Song und werden aufgefordert, ihr Grobverständnis mitzuteilen.
Die 2. Aufgabe kann in Einzelarbeit durchgeführt werden, jeder Schüler/jede Schülerin darf ein Zitat auswählen und anschließend im Plenum oder in der Gruppe erklären.
Die Fragen 3–6 sollten nicht unbedingt sukzessiv abgearbeitet werden, sondern vielmehr als Leitfragen gesehen werden, um eine nachvollziehbare Botschaft anhand des Songtextes herauszukristallisieren. Die Fragen könnten also zunächst stichpunktartig in einer Stillarbeitsphase angegangen werden, um darauf aufbauend im Plenum eine Botschaft textgeleitet zu diskutieren.
Die den Aufgabenapparat abschließende *Activity* 7 ist von den Schülerinnen und Schülern schriftlich zu lösen. Abhängig von der aktuellen Arbeitsbelastung der Lehrkraft, sollte den Schülerinnen und Schülern die Möglichkeit eröffnet werden, ihre Texte einzureichen. Es ist in diesem Zusammenhang empfehlenswert, die Lernenden zu befragen, wo ihr individueller Beratungsbedarf bzw. Förderbedarf liegt. Eigenverantwortlich sollten die Oberstufenschülerinnen und Oberstufenschüler der Lehrkraft nennen, worauf diese bei der Lektüre eines Textes ganz besonders achten und ein Feedback geben soll.

Solutions

Activities p. 40

1. **Ignoring the choruses for the moment, explain what the song is about in a few sentences.**
Mankind has arrived at the 'last century for man' but we are carrying on in the same old way, with the rich exploiting the poor, and the planet's resources, (so we have no hope of extending our stay on earth). The speaker/singer advises us to get in the car because that makes us happy, or become some kind of reality (TV) star. As it's our last century, we should consume all we possibly can while we have the chance.

2. **Tricky expressions. Try to explain what is meant by the following expressions:**
● **'If you are not outraged/You haven't been paying attention' (l. 6/7)**
Things are so bad that anyone who doesn't feel angry/furious just can't have been taking any interest in what is going on here on earth.
● **'Climb into the car/I know that makes you happy' (l. 15/16)**
As we have seen earlier in the unit, many people in our part of the world really love their cars (and people in developing countries who don't have cars yet, usually want one), so getting in the car to go for a ride makes people happy.
● **'Grace or disgrace/Can make you a star these days/Reality pays' (ll. 19–21)**
This is a reference to the celebrity-obsessed world we live in nowadays. It doesn't really matter whether you are a hero or a villain, the main thing is to become (temporarily) famous, appear in some kind of reality show on TV – and make a lot of money.
● **'Let's decide who the terrorists are' (l. 22)**
This is a reference to the fact that 'one man's terrorist is another man's freedom fighter'. There are several cases where people condemned as terrorists during unrest of some kind, later emerged as responsible politicians.
Unfortunately, Islamist terrorists (in our view) are celebrated as heroes by large numbers of people in Muslim countries. The line may also imply that people who destroy the environment could be considered as terrorists.

3. **The writer seems to be pretty sure that homo sapiens has entered his last century. What makes him so confident?**
He can see that exploitation (ll. 1–5) and consumption (ll. 28–32) are continuing unabated into this century, so the inevitable consequence is that we will wreck the planet in a relatively short time. There is no sign that we are taking the situation seriously.

4. **How far do you agree with him?**
Individual answers. Points that could be made:
Agree:
● global warming is accelerating
● energy consumption is rising
● pollution of all kinds is increasing
● desertification/flooding are both increasing
● resources are being exhausted
● rain forests are disappearing rapidly
● renewable resources still play a very minor role
Disagree:
● recycling is widespread for all kinds of materials
● cars are becoming cleaner/more economical
● no emissions from nuclear power plants (doubtful point)
● alternative forms of energy are gaining ground year by year
● large areas of the world are still relatively unspoilt

- the speaker/singer is overstating his case – things aren't (half) as bad as he claims
- the planet will find ways of defending itself/recovering, as it has done in the past (perhaps without homo sapiens)

5. **Comment on 'God bless America' and references to other countries mentioned in the choruses.**
These references can be seen as highly ironic. 'God Bless America' is a phrase often on the lips of American politicians, and it seems to imply that God is likely to do as he is told. It also implies a certain degree of self-satisfaction/complacency about America and its position in the world, its future etc. In the same way, the French like to refer to their country as 'la belle France'. The speaker/singer did not come up with anything for the UK, but of course he could have quoted Shakespeare on England, "This precious stone set in the silver sea ..." The speaker sees quotations of this kind as naive, because the pleasant state of affairs referred to is about to end in an environmental disaster.

6. **Discuss the singer's views on saving the planet.**
He makes it very clear that we have entered our last century, but he also encourages us to carry on consuming, perhaps in order to make the most of the time we have left. Students can try to decide if there is actually any point in making small individual savings which will not make any difference to the planet's future in the medium term. 'Let us eat, drink and be merry, for tomorrow we die!' (based on a biblical quotation from the book of Isaiah). He could also be trying to provoke us to disagree with him, along the following lines: "Just a minute, now. If we carry on as before/as suggested in the song, the end of the world will arrive even sooner."

7. **Although the writer clearly knows what we are doing wrong, he seems to be encouraging us to carry on in the same way. How far does this weaken the effect of the song? Write a paragraph on this topic, ending it with your own assessment of the song.**
Points that could be made:
   - Several points made above are also relevant here, e. g. making the most of the time we have left, little that individuals can do anyway, deliberate provocation.
   - The effect of the song is weakened if listeners/readers take 'Eat all we can', etc. at face value. Whether or not this is the case is for students to decide. Here are a couple of useful expressions:
     - Well, I can see why he says that, but ...
     - He shouldn't really be telling us to ...
     - I really go along with what he's saying.
     - It really makes you think about the issue.

   Further points:
   - Is this a protest song or not? I don't think the message is clear enough.
   - We do like doing all these things. There's no harm in it. Life should be fun.
   - Okay, 4 wheel drives are thirsty – but so what? Just think how much energy aeroplanes, factories and so on consume. What we use is just a drop in the ocean and won't make any difference to the fate of the planet.
   - I see it as a powerful warning – the style/tone of all these statements telling us what to do is clearly intended to make us stop and think whether it would really be a good idea to do as we are told in the song.

Worksheet 2

The Wind Farm – A Simulation

Imagine that a major wind farm is to be built at the edge of a village in the Welsh hills. Some people are in favour of it, others are against it. Work in groups of four and prepare for a debate in the Village Hall on the issue. Here are cue cards for the members of the group. Try to identify with your roles and make your case as strongly as possible. Don't just read out speeches – argue!

Farmer Evans

You have sold your land to the electricity company. You were not making a living from your farm any more, and have decided to give up farming altogether. Your son is a computer expert and has no interest in the farm. Your daughter has married and gone to live in another part of the country. You got a good price for your land, and you are pleased that you are indirectly doing something for the environment.

Mrs Jones,
local resident

Your garden borders on the big field where the wind generators are to be built. You believe in alternative energy, but not on your doorstep, so you are a NIMBY (not in my back yard). You are worried about noise as the big blades rotate, and shadows falling across your garden which may trigger one of your migraine attacks. Why not build wind farms out at sea where they won't bother people? A lot of your friends agree.

Mr. Jackson, manager,
electricity company,
not a local resident

You are very pleased to have obtained this excellent site for a wind farm. Until now your company has run a conventional power station, and you know the time has come to put the balance right by exploiting renewable power sources. You cannot understand why anyone would object – this is clean, almost silent power. Everyone benefits. No one suffers.

Samantha Crosby,
environmentalist

You are in a difficult position. Normally you would be in favour of alternative power, but when you saw the computer animation for this wind farm you were appalled. As a walker, you have often hiked across the field where the wind farm will be built, and the view would be completely ruined by dozens of huge wind generators. Surely there must be better ways of saving the environment.

Saving the Planet?

The Global Context

About the texts

This brief introductory material uses an environmentally friendly idea which could help to make ships more economical in order to illustrate what is perhaps the central problem with all isolated or individual attempts to save energy and protect the environment: what difference will my/their individual efforts make in a global context?

Unterrichtsempfehlungen

Die kleinen hinführenden Texte auf S. 41 zu dem Kapitel „Saving the Planet" sollten gemeinsam im Plenum gelesen werden. Auch die Activities können im Plenum besprochen werden und die Arbeit an den folgenden Texten, Bildern und Grafiken vorbereiten.

Solutions

Activities p. 41

1. **How does the Beluga save fuel?**
   It uses a giant kite-like/parachute-like sail to supplement its normal diesel engines. It may be able to reduce its fuel consumption (and CO_2 emissions) by 20% in normal service.

2. **What advantages and disadvantages of this system can you think of?**
   ⊕
   - Once the sail has been bought and set up, there are no further costs.
   - 20% less energy consumption is a really significant amount when we consider how much fuel ships burn (compared with the airline industry).
   - If a lot of ships started to use this system, there could be really major savings.

   ⊖
   - There isn't always enough wind.
   - It doesn't always come from the right direction.
   - Possible technical problems with such a large sail.
   - 20% could well turn out to be too optimistic/may only be achieved under ideal conditions.

Shipping Boom Increases CO_2 Emissions

John Vidal

Photograph

The photograph shows a typical giant container ship belonging to the Danish Maersk Line, one of the world's largest shipping companies.

Background information

Until quite recently hardly anyone has worried about emissions from ships, which tend to be seen as somehow cleaner than other forms of transport, and well away from bothering us on land anyway. This article sets the record straight.

Unterrichtsempfehlungen

Die Aufgabe 1 *The facts* sollte nach der Lektüre in einer Stillarbeitsphase von jeder Schülerin und jedem Schüler gelöst werden. Die im Rahmen dieser Aufgabe zu erstellende Liste kann dann in Kleingruppen auf Vollständigkeit hin überprüft werden. Auch die zwei Aufgaben zu *A fair comparison?* können zunächst in einer Gruppenarbeitsphase angegangen werden. Während die Ergebnisse zu Nr. 2 in einem offenen Unterrichtsgespräch beleuchtet und an der Tafel stichpunktartig (*several relevant points* – vgl. *Solutions*) festgehalten werden sollten, können Argumente zur Beantwortung der 3. Aufgabe in einem offenen Unterrichtsgespräch kontrovers diskutiert werden.

Solutions

Activities p. 42

1. Make a straightforward list of the main points in the article

- The world's largest merchant/container ship burns nearly 350 tonnes of fuel a day on its way from China to Europe.
- This adds up to more than 300,000 tonnes of CO_2 a year – as much as a medium-sized coal power station.
- Reducing emissions is not a priority for shipowners or governments.
- The world shipping fleet emits 1.21 billion tonnes a year, or nearly 4.5 % of world emissions.
- Whereas the aviation industry is under pressure to clean up its act, the much higher global emissions from shipping have hardly been noticed (until recently).

2. To what extent is it fair to compare ships with aeroplanes in the pollution stakes? You should be able to make several relevant points.

- The actual volume of goods carried on ships is far higher than for aeroplanes – we would have to work out pollution per tonne of goods carried to have a fair comparison.
- Emissions from ships are less likely to rise into the upper atmosphere.
- People living near ports don't usually complain about air/noise pollution; people living near airports have every reason to complain – and do so on a regular basis.
- Pollution from ships is less obvious generally, but the actual quantities are larger.

3. Why do you think that shipping has escaped the attention of environmentalists until fairly recently, whereas flying has come in for a lot of criticism?

See the last two points above. As ships spend most of their time out on the oceans, we just don't see the pollution taking place. At airports and above our heads, it's obvious.

Ships have a nicer, more romantic, even cleaner image, which, as we now know, is deceptive.

Planes are perhaps an easier target for environmentalists, as people who fly often have a bad conscience (see SB p. 37–38), whereas the crews of merchant ships (and even passengers on cruise ships) probably don't worry about the environmental effects of their mode of transport at all.

Islanders Turned Green

David Lister

Photograph and drawings

The photograph shows the idyllic, but also rather lonely landscape on the Scottish island of Eigg. The drawing on p. 43 illustrates the problems which will still exist when Eigg has its own power supply. Ordinary householders will only be allocated 5 kilowatts, which means people can't turn all their household appliances on at the same time, and will have to do the 'electric chores' one after another.
The drawing on p. 44 shows what will happen if they turn on everything at once.

Unterrichtsempfehlungen

Die Lektüre des Textes und die Erstellung der Fragen im Rahmen der ersten Aufgabe erfolgt als Hausaufgabe. Der zweiten Aufgabenstellung folgend werden die formulierten Fragen dann zusammen mit einem Partner beantwortet und zur Abfassung einer *summary* herangezogen.
Die Aufgaben 3 und 4 sollten zunächst kurz in einem Unterrichtsgespräch besprochen werden, aus dem einige Ansätze, eine erste Orientierung hervorgehen. Die Schülerinnen und Schüler sollten während des Unterrichtsgespräches Notizen anfertigen. Als Hausaufgabe sollte dann von den Schülerinnen und Schülern eine Vertiefung vorgenommen werden, die u. a. auf Nachforschung, Recherche beruht. *It's an emotional issue* lädt insbesondere mit der Aufgabe 5 zu szenischem Spiel, zur Erstellung eines Dialogs ein. Die Bearbeitung der Aufgaben 6 und 7 hilft diesbezüglich zu einer Annäherung an die Menschen der Insel und trägt zur Vertiefung interkultureller Kompetenzen bei. Die den Aufgabenapparat abschließende Aufgabe ist in schriftlicher Form zu lösen.

Solutions

Activities p. 44

1. **Write a set of questions, the answers to which would tell someone who hasn't read the text what it is about.**
   (Most people would begin with a very general introductory sentence before going on to the detailed questions, e. g. This text is about supplying a small island with reliable electricity.)
   1. Where is this island?
   2. How many people live there?
   3. Am I right in thinking that they are going to produce/generate their own electricity?
   4. How will it be done?
   5. How did they make electricity in the past?
   6. What will be different for them now?
   7. How do they feel about their new electricity supply?
   8. Why will they have to be careful about their electricity consumption?
   9. Who is paying for the new scheme?
   10. Why didn't they just lay a cable under the sea (from the Scottish mainland)?
2. **Work with a partner to answer the questions and turn them into a summary of the text.**
   1. The island is off the coast of Scotland.
   2. 87 people
   3. Yes, you are/that's right.

4. They will use a combination of wind, hydro-electric power and solar power. The electricity will be distributed to 60 houses and businesses via an island-wide grid.
5. They had unreliable diesel generators which pumped out clouds of black smoke.
6. They will have (nearly) all the advantages of mains electricity.
7. They are really delighted, and proud of the fact that the scheme uses only renewable sources of energy.
8. Because normal households will only be allocated five kilowatts, which means that they cannot turn everything on at once.
9. Funds have been contributed by the islanders themselves, by the EU, the National Lottery, and a Scottish energy company.
10. The islanders decided on this solution because laying a cable from the mainland would have been too expensive.

Summary
This text is about supplying a small island with reliable electricity. The island is called Eigg, and it is off the coast of Scotland. Eighty-seven people live there, and they decided to make their electricity themselves, using a combination of wind, hydro-electric power and solar power. The electricity is distributed to 60 houses and businesses via an island-wide grid. In the past, electricity on Eigg was produced by unreliable diesel generators which pumped out clouds of black smoke. From now on the islanders will have nearly all the advantages of mains electricity, but they will have to be careful not to turn on everything at once, because normal households will only be allocated five kilowatts. Funds for the scheme were contributed by the islanders themselves, and by various national and international bodies. The islanders decided on this solution because a cable from the mainland would have been too expensive. They are really delighted with the scheme, and proud of the fact that it uses only renewable sources of energy.
Note: Some of the points from the text have been rearranged in the summary, to link similar items, avoid repetition (e. g. the list of energy sources), and provide a suitable conclusion.
Students should be encouraged to experiment with rearranging the material in the same way.

3. **Why would this solution not be feasible for larger areas?**
   It would be difficult to produce enough energy from renewable sources for large, densely-populated areas.

4. **Do you know of a fairly large country which produces nearly all its energy from renewable sources? How do they do it?**
   The best example near at hand is Norway, which has ample supplies of hydroelectric power (and sells its offshore oil to other, less fortunate countries, with enviable results for the economy).

5. **Imagine you are one of the islanders talking to a visitor. Explain how you feel about the new electricity supply.**
   An example:
   Well, (Joyce), it's just fantastic. I turn on the light and the light comes on. Every time! Look! I suppose you take that for granted over there in Dundee. Well, we don't, I can tell you. We never knew when one of the generators was going to break down and leave us in the dark. And we lost all the stuff in the freezer several times because of power failures. We'll get used to all this luxury in time, I suppose, but for the moment it's great. And we did it all ourselves. Well, not me personally, of course, but the is-

landers made the decision, got it all planned, arranged the finance and so on. We're really proud of ourselves. Sorry if that sounds a big big-headed.

6. Comment on the use of direct speech in the article.

When we read what the lady who runs the shop, and the wife of the chairman of Eigg Electricity actually say about the change in their lives, we can share their enthusiasm. As all students working with the text (and readers of the newspaper from which it was taken) are likely to have taken mains electricity for granted all their lives, we are likely to wonder what all the fuss is about on Eigg. Direct speech helps us to 'get the message'.

7. What kind of people do the islanders seem to be?

Some ideas:

friendly, chatty, resourceful, independent, prepared to put up with hardships, but almost childishly enthusiastic about their new electricity supply and the fact that it is environmentally friendly

8. Nearly everyone in the developed world takes a reliable electricity supply for granted. How do you think your family would manage if there was a long-term power cut (or outage, as the Americans say)?

Some questions to get students thinking:

- Torch/candles somewhere where you can find them in the dark?
- Some kind of stove to provide heat if there is no central heating?
- Entertainment?
- Communication with the outside world (no phones, batteries in mobiles will soon be flat)?
- Hot water for showers, cooking, washing up?
- Is there a gas grill in the house with an independent gas supply? Could be quite useful.

State of Fear (1st extract)

Michael Crichton

About the author

Michael Crichton was born in Chicago and educated at Harvard Medical School. His novels often combine scientific and action themes. He became world-famous after Jurassic Park was made into a film which enjoyed tremendous popularity. As well as *State of Fear*, *The Andromeda Strain* and *Prey* are well worth reading.

Unterrichtsempfehlungen

Die Lektüre des kurzen Romanauszuges und die Bearbeitung der Aufgaben 1 und 2 sollten in Stillarbeit vorgenommen werden. Dabei sollte die erste Aufgabe zu einem vollständigen Text, einer *summary* führen, während die Aufgabe 2 stichpunktartig gelöst werden kann.

Für den Umgang mit der 3. Aufgabe ist es empfehlenswert, dass die Lehrkraft die *statements* von Evans im Vorfeld herausarbeitet und gut lesbar auf eine Folie für den OHP druckt. Zum einen wird so eine Visualisierung, eine konkretere Bezugs- und Kommentierungsmöglichkeit geschaffen, zum anderen wird die zunehmende Skepsis Evans auf diese Weise „plastisch".

Die 3 Aufgaben zu *Who is right?* sollten von den Schülerinnen und Schülern zu Hause vorbereitet werden. Im Unterricht können dann Ergebnisse ausgetauscht und auf ihre Stichhaltigkeit in Kleingruppen überprüft werden. Diese Phase der Kleingruppenarbeit

sollte zu Ergebnisprotokollen führen, die von der Lehrkraft eingesammelt und ausgewertet werden können. Nachfolgend kann die Lehrkraft in einem Lehrervortrag die überzeugendsten Aspekte aus den Protokollen bündeln. Ebenfalls ist bei dieser Gelegenheit an *focus on form – accuracy* zu denken, bei der die Lehrkraft im Sinne einer Profilbildung vorgeht.
Die den Aufgabenapparat abschließende Aufgabe (Nr. 10) ist in einer kurzen Stillarbeitsphase vorzubereiten. Danach sollte sie gründlich im Rahmen eines erarbeitenden Unterrichtsgespräches angegangen werden. Grundsätzliches zum Umgang mit Grafiken muss dabei beachtet werden. Eine vergrößerte Kopie der Grafiken auf eine Folie (oder mithilfe von Laptop und Beamer) ist für den Arbeitsprozess sinnvoll.

Solutions

Activities p. 46

1. Summarise what the weather report says about climate change.
Points made:
- More extreme weather events caused by global warming.
- Greenland glaciers will soon vanish entirely.
- Sea levels may rise by 20 feet or more.

2. How does Kenner react?
- He points out that the weather report is simply a press release from some other source.
- He claims that the information in it is not true.
- He says that there is no increase in extreme weather.
- He quotes studies which say that global warming may result in less extreme weather.
- He points out that Greenland might lose its ice pack in the next thousand years, not 'soon', as stated by the weatherman.

Note: Students may wonder why a weather report on a news programme would include sensational and misleading material. The answer is surely that news, including the weather news, has to be entertaining, and sensational stuff is generally more entertaining than the facts. The news is also a 'show'.

3. Go through the extract and pick out statements by Evans which show how his views are becoming more sceptical. Comment briefly on each statement.
- 'This guy is just reading a press release?' (l. 8)

(Evans would have assumed in the past that the weather people, meteorologists, would have done their own homework.)
- 'Then what's causing the increase in extreme weather around the world?' (l. 12)

(Evans takes it for granted that there is an increase in extreme weather, because this has become the conventional wisdom/this is what he reads in the newspapers.)
- 'So he's just full of shit?' (l. 19)

(He no longer takes what the weather man is saying seriously.)
- 'What about that one? [the melting ice pack in Greenland] It was on the news in LA yesterday.' (l. 26)

(Evans is still prepared to believe news items but now he knows in advance that he should question what he hears on the radio or TV, or reads in the newspapers.)

4. Explain how the weatherman has distorted the original press release.
The weather man reads out the first part of the press release verbatim, but makes significant changes in the second part, which Kenner corrects:
- will – might

- soon – next thousand years
- no mention at all of a thousand years in the report

5. **What do you know about the Greenland ice pack? (See pages 15–17)**
(Plenty of information available.) Some points to make:
- Sudden changes in climate have taken place in the past, with dramatic consequences for the ice sheet.
- The previous interglacial period was somewhat warmer than the present one (so far).
- Sea levels rose 15 feet.
- There is some thickening at the centre of the sheet, but it is shrinking by twelve cubic miles per year.

6. **List some aspects of global warming which you have read about or seen discussed on TV. How far was the information convincing?**
Mainly individual work. Students may have heard about any of the following. They should be encouraged to find out about local aspects if possible.
- different migration patterns for birds
- species extending their habitats further north
- southern plants growing further north (vines in Schleswig-Holstein)
- warmer summers
- less reliable weather
- rising water levels/threats to coastal communities
- water shortages/desertification

7. **In the light of your previous answer, try to decide whether Kenner is right to be so sceptical.**
- Crichton published *State of Fear* in 2004. If he was writing the book in 2003, his views will have been based on the situation fairly early in the century.
- Since then global warming trends have become more marked.
- However, Kenner, probably speaking for Crichton, wants to point out that trends are not consistent all over the world, and that there is a tendency for media people to exaggerate and select information to make their reports more interesting.

8. **Have a look at the following statistics. New York and Albany are in the same state. How could the temperature in New York have risen while the temperature in Albany has fallen slightly during the period covered?**
This is exactly the kind of information which Kenner/Crichton feels that people should be given. We would tend to accept the New York graph as typical for the general trend, but apparently the trend is by no means clear.
The most likely reasons for the rise in temperature in New York are that cities generally get hotter than the countryside, and that traffic densities/energy consumption will have risen during a period of prosperity. Out in the country, it is likely that forests will have helped to keep temperatures down.

State of Fear (2nd extract)

Background information

In the second extract Crichton is exploring a paradox. The very people who are most active in trying to make people aware of the dangers of global warming are likely to cover a great many air and road miles, so their personal carbon footprint is likely to be much larger than average. It's a case of not 'practising what you preach'.

How Not To Be Green kann im Sinne der Aufgabenstellungen so für alle Schülerinnen und Schüler visualisierend und im Verlauf des Unterrichtsgespräches bearbeitet werden.
Die Aufgabe 5 ist von jeder Schülerin und jedem Schüler in Einzelarbeit zu erledigen und dient der intensiven Vorbereitung des *role play* (Nr. 6).
Es ist möglich, noch weitere Gesprächspartner hinzuzufügen, um einen lebendigen „Schlagabtausch" in Szene zu setzen. Es ist sehr empfehlenswert, die vor dem Plenum präsentierten Szenen zu filmen. Eine vielschichtige und funktionale Auswertung hinsichtlich inhaltlicher Argumentation, der Sprache und auch Darstellungsform sind wünschenswert.
Für die Abfassung des *essays* (Nr. 7) sollte den Schülerinnen und Schülern ein überschaubarer Zeitraum zur Verfügung gestellt werden, der eine gründliche und intensive Auseinandersetzung möglich macht. Die Lehrerin/der Lehrer sollte dann die Texte der Kursmitglieder einsammeln, lesen und ihnen im Sinne der individuellen Förderung differenziert ein kurzes Feedback geben.

Solutions

Before you read p. 49

Can you point out some of the inconsistencies in the drawing below?
The wife is replacing a normal light-bulb with a low-energy one, but otherwise her kitchen is full of electrical equipment. Relatively speaking, only a tiny amount of energy will be saved by changing the bulb. It would be far more effective to throw out any one of the other appliances. However, we can assume that the prosperous wife in the picture likes all her electrical goodies, so she is unlikely to do anything of the kind. So she changes a bulb instead in an attempt to silence her conscience.
If students read that the husband works for an environmental agency, they will point out that he shouldn't be driving to work in an SUV.

Activities p. 50

1. **Make a list of the kinds of behaviour and items referred to in the article, and try to decide whether they are 'green', somewhat green or not green at all.**
   - Husband drives an SUV to work (not green).
     (Pointless to drive a thirsty SUV in town, where a small car would be more suitable in every respect.)
   - Walking to work (green).
   - Taking the bus (somewhat green or green).
     (A bus takes 40+ people, but only uses as much fuel as 3 or 4 cars.)
   - Leaving electrical equipment on standby (not green).
     (Not much electricity used, but it's completely unnecessary – total waste.)
   - Not recycling (not green).
     (Recycling means that materials can be used again in some form instead of ending up on rubbish tips/landfill sites or in incinerators.)
   - Cooking on a (coal-fired) Aga (not green).
     (Coal is a fossil fuel. Burning it produces smoke and CO_2, and of course fossil fuels are not replaceable.)
   - Wife wanted the SUV (not green).
     (We can safely assume she would have wanted it for status reasons although this kind of car is unnecessary for at least 80 % of the population – farmers and caravanners can be excused.)
   - Won't wear a jersey (in the house, implied, so the heating has to be turned up high, not green).
     (He could wear a jersey and turn down the heating to save energy.)
   - Wife leaves Blackberry charger on (not green – but the amount of electricity used would be negligible).

– Husband buys cheapo fruit (not very green – organic ('bio) would of course be green).
– Husband brings stuff home in lots of packaging and plastic bags (not green). (Packaging and plastic bags are usually made from oil – there are some alternatives made from cellulose – and many of them end up on rubbish tips or blowing around the countryside/injuring or killing animals.)
– Eating animals (not very green – could be discussed). (It takes a lot more grain to feed beef cattle than it does to feed people if they eat products made directly from the grain.)
– Wearing leather (a non-synthetic material, but some poor animal died to supply it – possibly not really a green issue).
– Holidaying in Britain or abroad (at home is greener than abroad). (Energy consumed is going to be less for a holiday at home.)
– Going by car or train (train is greener – if there is a station anywhere near, that is). (As with the bus versus car debate, a train uses far less energy than the same number of people travelling in cars.)

2. **For the somewhat green and not green at all items, explain why they could be considered lacking in 'greenness'.**
(See notes above)

3. **How do we know that there is a lot of media interest in Mr Dawnay's idea? Why might that be?**
He has been telephoned by a broadsheet journalist.
Receives a call from the (highly respected) Radio 4 Today programme.
We can assume that there is interest in his ideas for the environment because nearly everyone has a bad conscience and would like to 'do better' in environmental terms, as long as it doesn't affect our lifestyle too much.

4. **What evidence is there for saying that the couple featured here are middle-class or above?**
   - Rachel Johnson writes for *The Sunday Times* – a respected broadsheet newspaper.
   - Her husband obviously has an important job which will be well paid.
   - Honest workers don't have names like Ivo Dawnay.
   - The Volvo
   - The Aga
   - The espresso machine

5. **Make a personal list similar to the one in activity 2 above, and explain why you still indulge in some activities which are not as green as they might be.**
Plenty of activities are mentioned above. Some typical excuses?
Pure laziness, don't like energy-saving light-bulbs, don't like (very) small cars – no fun driving them, see no reason not to fly to holiday destinations, 'everybody' does it, re-cycling is sometimes just too much bother – don't believe they actually re-cycle everything anyway (students may have seen TV programmes which show that a lot of plastic, for example, goes on to rubbish tips or gets incinerated).

6. **Role-play: Work in pairs. One of you pretends to be ultra-green, and the other pretends to be an unreformed character who sees nothing much wrong with flying, thirsty cars, non-organic food, plastic bags for everything and so on. Practise and perform a lively argument.**
Plenty of material has been provided. Possible starter:
A: So you're off to Majorca again in the summer, are you?
B: So what?

A: Well, planes burn a lot of fuel.
B: How much less would 'my' plane burn if I wasn't on board?
A: That's not the point.
B: What is the point, then?

7. **Write a short essay in which you outline your own policy on environmental issues, and also suggest some steps which you think the government should be taking to 'save the planet'.**
(Individual work, guidance given in the SB)
Some useful expressions:
- In my view, ...
- On the whole I (tend to) think ...
- I have thought about this issue a lot, and come to the conclusion that ...
- Perhaps we worry too much about ...
- I don't see how an individual/a single country can really make a difference, because ...
- I'm really concerned about ...
- On balance I feel that ...
- If I had the power to change things, I would ban/change/reduce/develop ...

Spiralling towards Destruction

Elizabeth Kolbert

Unterrichtsempfehlungen

Die Einführung (S. 51 oben) zu den kleinen, jedoch gehaltvollen Texten sollte gemeinsam im Plenum gelesen werden. Die vertiefende Arbeit mit den Texten und den dazugehörigen Aufgaben kann dann der Kugellagermethode folgend auf die Kursmitglieder verteilt werden (zur Methode des Kugellagers – *double circle* – vgl. Schöningh, Method Guide 5–10). Die Methode des *double circle* fördert nicht nur den autonom handelnden Lerner, sondern ermöglicht einen Unterrichtsprozess mit sehr hohen Sprechanteilen auf Seiten der Schülerinnen und Schülern. Im Anschluss daran sollte ein offenes Unterrichtsgespräch geführt werden, bei dem die Schülerinnen und Schüler zu dem Problem „Are we spiralling towards destruction?" Stellung beziehen, einander zuhören und aufeinander reagieren. Die Lehrkraft sollte dabei darauf achten, dass die Schülerinnen und Schüler argumentativ vorgehen, sich auf die Texte beziehen und zentrale Punkte aus dem Gespräch notieren. Als Hausaufgabe sollte dann jede Schülerin und jeder Schüler seine Position verschriftlichen.

Solutions

Activities p. 53

1. **How does the 'good' effect of greenhouse gases work?**
Greenhouse gases limit the outward flow of infra-red energy (heat) so that the average global temperature is 57° Fahrenheit (14 °C). Without greenhouse gases it would be 0° F (–18 °C).

2. **What would life on earth be like without these gases?**
There would either be no life at all, or only forms adapted to very low temperatures. Probably the whole surface of the planet would be covered with ice.

3. **And what are the familiar bad effects?**
As a result of increasing quantities of greenhouse gases, the planet is getting warmer, with melting ice-caps, rising sea-levels, and climate change making temperate areas hotter.

4. **The writer could not find even *one* scientist who thought global warming was a natural process. What does this tell us?**
It tells us that the people who ought to know believe that global warming is taking place (at an alarming rate), and that our species is responsible for it.

5. **What point is the writer making in connection with the "megaspecies"?**
She points out that although these species survived various glacial cycles, at some point they nearly all died out as a result of some change which they could not adapt to.

6. **Why has she made this point?**
She wants us to realise that the same thing could happen to homo sapiens.

7. **What is particularly worrying about the present warming process?**
If the present warming process continues, by the end of the century we will be in unknown territory. Temperatures will have risen beyond any of the natural temperature variations of the past.

8. **What does the ice core record tell us about temperatures on earth and carbon dioxide levels?** Activities p. 54
It tells us that both temperatures and CO_2 levels will reach levels completely beyond human experience unless we manage to reverse the trends.

9. **Why should this information worry us?**
Because life as we know it (and it is a pretty nice life for most of us, when we consider what conditions are like on other planets) will change in ways we cannot predict, and possibly cannot adapt to.

10. **Dobriansky was trying to explain and justify her government's refusal to sign the Kyoto protocol. Did she do a good job? Give reasons for your answer.**
Dobriansky keeps using the word 'serious(ly)', and repeating herself in other ways too, in the hope that listeners will be impressed, but in fact she does not list a single strategy which would slow down climate change, or say anything at all which has any real meaning. We would have to say that she does a terrible job. However, it may not be her fault. Most observers believe that George W. Bush's energy policies were indefensible.

11. **How would you describe this kind of talk? Use examples from the extract to support your views.**
The extract is typical of the way in which some politicians or officials talk – using a lot of rather pretentious words without actually saying anything, e. g. 'let me just add, in terms of, not only stating to you, engaged ... in initiatives, the bottom line here, a common goal and initiative, different approaches'. The words 'jargon' and 'gobbledygook' can be used to describe this kind of language.

12. **How are the Chinese planning to meet their huge and growing energy demands?**
By building hundreds of new coal-burning power stations (they are experimenting with cleaner technologies, but still intend to burn coal for the foreseeable future).

13. **Why is the rest of the world worried?**
Because the huge amounts of carbon produced by these new (and old) coal-burning power stations completely swamp/dwarf/outweigh efforts by other countries to save energy.

14. Do we (in the developed world) have the right to criticise the Chinese? Give reasons for your answer.

When other countries industrialised, they also used dirty technologies in the early stages, and western countries (plus Japan and Australia) consume far more energy than the Chinese, person for person, so to some extent we should be tolerant towards the Chinese. Otherwise it would be a case of 'the pot calling the kettle black', or 'people in glass houses should not throw stones.' However, the huge amount of carbon produced by China is a danger for everyone, the Chinese included, so it is in everyone's interests for them to reduce their carbon emissions. The problem is, how? They will hardly be prepared to accept restrictions from outside, and CCS technology (carbon capture and storage) for CO_2 is still in its infancy. Atomic power is no longer seen as a clean source of power, and alternative energy forms cannot deliver the quantities required at present.

China does seem to be genuinely concerned about its carbon footprint. Perhaps they will take a lead in developing clean technologies for coal.

15. Was there any point in Burlington's efforts to save energy (and similar projects elsewhere) in view of what is likely to happen on the energy front in China?

We have to admit that small-scale savings of the kind achieved in Burlington are just a drop in the ocean. We have to hope that good examples of this kind will persuade other communities/countries to set out along the same track. However, even if the Chinese government has heard of Burlington, we can safely assume that Burlington's efforts will not influence their energy policies.

16. How could China reduce its energy requirements?

- alternative forms of energy
- new, more efficient factories, heating systems etc.
- find ways of cleaning up coal-fired power stations.
- cutting production (this was happening at the time of writing as a result of the global depression)

17. Do you think there is any likelihood of this reduction actually taking place?

As the world economy picks up, we can safely assume that energy requirements will rise again. It is possible to imagine that the curve will flatten out as China modernises its factories and power stations, but an actual reduction in energy requirements is unlikely.

18. What is ironic about China's production of energy-saving lighting?

They make most of the world's energy-saving bulbs, but they hardly use any themselves.

19. When a scientist starts talking like a science fiction author, should we take him seriously or not? Think about the point he is making, and write a paragraph about the future of our species as you see it.

The scientist certainly means what he says, and we should take him seriously, even if the scenario he describes sounds like science fiction.

Students should be encouraged to refer to SF sources they know, where the demise of our species is described (e.g. Cormac McCarthy, *The Road*, 2006). The scenario is often post-nuclear-disaster, as in *The Road*, rather than hot/dry/flooded/contaminated earth, but this is becoming all too easy to imagine.

The best hope for optimists is for us to find ways of harnessing really large amounts of the sun's energy.

20. What might survive if we don't?

The smart money is on rats, insects, micro-organisms. Not a very attractive prospect.

News Flashes

About the texts

The book ends with a series of short texts about various aspects of the environment, providing a kaleidoscope of facts and ideas for students to think about before they move on to other topics.

Unterrichtsempfehlungen

Die Lehrkraft sollte die Bearbeitung von „News Flashes“ als eine Art Wochenaufgabe konzipieren, bei der die Schülerinnen und Schüler in Partnerarbeit vorgehen. Die Partnerarbeit sollte jedoch nicht im Unterricht stattfinden, sondern von den Lernern als Hausaufgabe geleistet werden. Dabei sollen die Partner dazu angehalten werden, sich in Freistunden, in Phasen des eigenverantwortlichen Lernens (EVA) oder aber per E-Mail intensiv auszutauschen und im Sinne der Fragen am Rand der Texte/Aussagen zu Ergebnissen zu gelangen. Diese sollten dann auf die Problemstellung „And finally ... Will we change our ways in time to save the planet (and our pleasant life-styles) or is it already too late?“ auf einem Plakat strukturiert und ansprechend festgehalten werden. Ein weiteres leeres Plakat sollte Schülerinnen und Schüler eines Parallelkurses oder eines Englischkurses einer anderen Jahrgangsstufe zu Kommentaren in der Zielsprache anregen. Es ist die organisatorische Aufgabe der Lehrkraft, mit einer Kollegin/einem Kollegen eines anderen Englischkurses in Kontakt zu treten, um dies in angemessener Form zu ermöglichen und in Gang zu setzen.
Ein Gespräch, das die Kommentare der Schülerinnen und Schüler des anderen Kurses zur Grundlage hat, kann den Prozess abrunden.

Solutions

The plastic bag menace, p. 54

Ask your own questions – and ask your partner to answer them.

- e.g. Why do we use so many plastic bags? (convenience/cheap or free)
- Why aren't more bags recycled in Britain? (don't care enough)
- Do you accept free plastic bags – or take your own bag when you go shopping?
- What are plastic bags made of? (oil, occasionally cellulose)

The green land grab, p. 55

1. **How do you think the local people feel when they find out that their land has been bought by foreigners or outsiders?**
   Angry, powerless, amazed that this is possible.
2. **Are the new owners likely to treat the land better than the locals?**
   If we are honest, the new owners will probably save rain forests, for example, from destruction (see SB p. 11). In western countries, the buying up of attractive land is likely to lead to PRIVATE – KEEP OUT signs and/or housing developments/hotels for the wealthy.
3. **How would carbon credits work? How could the landbuyers benefit?**
   Poor countries could sell the carbon in their trees to rich countries, giving the rich countries the 'right' to go on polluting – a morally very questionable practice. The new landowners could also sell carbon credits in this way, and no doubt intend to do so, so their claim to be protecting the environment is really motivated by self-interest.

"Grand Slam" p. 55

1. **Who is he, and what do you know about him?**
   He is Al Gore, American democratic politician, unsuccessful presidential candidate (against George W. Bush), and environmentalist.

Bio-fuels – are they the answer?
pro: renewable, carbon neutral
con: hard to produce sufficient quantities, food crops may suffer, possible technical problems with conventional car engines
Carbon capture for conventional power stations?
pro: would solve the problem of CO_2 emissions in the medium term
con: no commercial scheme yet functioning, protests from people who are threatened with (liquefied) gas deposits under their feet – no one knows if this is likely to be dangerous
Wind turbines – the perfect source of power?
pro: no pollution
con: no wind – no electricity, huge areas need to be turned into wind farms to produce really significant amounts of power
protests from local people (noise, shadows, views ruined) and environmentalists (ugly blots on the landscape), wind farms out at sea may be a danger to shipping/damage fishing grounds
Global meltdown as oil runs out?
pro: Oil wars possible, also the world's wheels may gradually stop turning, with consequences no one can really predict.
con: We are an adaptable species – will find alternatives before it is too late (although we will need to adapt quickly as energy consumption rises rapidly in huge, dynamic economies such as India and China – this is probably the greatest challenge our species has had to face, and so far we are still on the road to disaster). The need to adapt has never been so urgent before – from coal to oil (no problem) from oil to ...? We don't have a convincing answer yet.
There's lots of energy in the sea, isn't there?
pro: Tidal barrages can harness energy as sea levels rise and fall. Wave energy can also be harnessed, no pollution.
con: Applications limited to coastal areas with suitable conditions. Major environmental changes when tidal estuaries/bays are dammed.
The industrial nations are just too selfish and greedy.
pro: We consume far more energy per head of population than India, for example, and we will not give up our high standards of living without a struggle.
con: Most of the main efforts to save energy and develop clean power have so far been in the industrial countries, with America beginning to join in now that the Bush era is over.
Never mind the oil running out – the real problems are desertification and food shortages.
pro: Hundreds of thousand of people, especially children, die of starvation and disease every year, mainly in parts of Africa.
con: There are huge aid programmes financed by the rich countries, but they cannot prevent humanitarian disasters, particularly in war zones. We can only try to save as many people as possible, but as most of them will be living in camps, they have no hope of becoming self-sufficient again as they have no means of support.

Worksheet 3

It Is Not Hypocritical[1] to Fly If I'm Campaigning for the Environment

Trudie Styler

Given the Guardian's reputation for a positive stance on the environment, I was angered and saddened by the cheap and scathing[2] tone of your "Lost in showbiz" article about me (Trudie Styler: "Saving the world one private jet flight at a time", 15 May, 2009).

It sought to demolish my credibility as an environmental campaigner by laying charges[3] of hypocrisy against my readily admitted occasional use of private aviation fuel as well as many (less reported) flights on scheduled commercial flights. The article's gripe[4] extended to a sour attempt to create some sort of faux[5] class envy around me in seeking to "focus ... on madam's most cherished[6] public pose: that of eco warrior".

The piece turned on the curious assertion that "Trudie's lifestyle compromises[7] her environmental message so fatally that she can only be a big oil double agent created ... with the sole aim of undermining an important message with her rank[8] hypocrisy". Ironically the publication of this article, with its unsustainable attack on my integrity, actually casts the Guardian in the role of double agent. You have given succour[9] to what I would have assumed was a mutual foe[10], the Chevron oil company[11].

For many years much of my work as an environmental campaigner has focused on exposing the devastation caused to large parts of Ecuador by Chevron during its exploitation of drilling rights. The recent documentary, *Crude*, in which I played a substantial role, has effectively concentrated global opposition to Chevron's continued refusal to make proper recompense[12] for damage to thousands of lives.

Your article will be invaluable to those working on behalf of Chevron who seek to undermine this 14-year campaign through attacking my reputation.

Of course I use aeroplanes. Even the most dogmatic and dictatorial advocates[13] of environmental reform would be hard pressed[14] to suggest that Ecuador (and, yes, Washington) are practical places to reach by wagon train or boat.

Each year I fly thousands of miles to campaign for environmental change. It would have been inconceivable to raise tens of millions of pounds for the Rainforest Foundation – which protects the forests and their indigenous[15] people and of which I was a joint founder 21 years ago – on horseback. It would have been similarly impracticable to have served as a global Unicef ambassador on a bicycle.

---

1 **hypocritical** pretending to be different from what one really is
2 **scathing** harsh, severe
3 **to lay charges against sth.** to say that sth. is wrong
4 **gripe** complaint
5 **faux** incorrect
6 **cherished** loved
7 **to compromise** *here* to make weak
8 **rank** adj., derog. complete
9 **succour** help for sb. in need
10 **foe** enemy
11 **Chevron oil company** one of the world's biggest oil companies
12 **recompense** *Entschädigung*
13 **advocate** sb. in favour of sth.
14 **be hard pressed** to have difficulties in achieving sth.
15 **indigenous** native

Worksheet 3

I am fortunate to receive occasional access to world leaders and those who can influence and implement environmental change. Hence trips to affluent world capitals as well as lands laid waste[16] by the environmental vandals.

The Global Canopy Programme, an alliance of leading scientists, says one day's deforestation equates to the carbon footprint[17] of 8 million people flying from London to New York.

According to Nicholas Stern, over the next four years alone the destruction of forests in the Amazon, the Congo basin and Indonesia will pump more CO_2 into the atmosphere than every flight in the history of aviation to 2025.

Being criticised for devoting large amounts of my time and our (earned) money to a cause which offends so many vested interests is an occupational hazard. But to be so undermined by the Guardian, albeit[18] on its showbiz pages, feels like being hit by a particularly vicious burst of friendly fire[19].

Trudie Styler: "It Is Not Hypocritical to Fly If I'm Campaigning for the Environment", in: The Guardian, May 22, 2009, © Guardian News & Media Ltd 2009

[16]**laid waste** completely destroyed
[17]**carbon footprint** the amount of carbon set free by an individual, organisation, event or product
[18]**albeit** although
[19]**friendly fire** an attack by one's own side

Activities

1. **Trudie Styler was attacked in *The Guardian* for flying huge distances on environmental missions. *The Guardian* offers a 'right of reply' and Ms. Styler exercised this right. Work in pairs. One of you collects points in Ms. Styler's favour, the other looks for weaknesses in her case.**

2. **Was *The Guardian's* attack fair? Does she really need to travel around in a private jet? Is she doing a good job, or is she mainly interested in her reputation as an environmentalist? Discuss the issue in a confrontational way, then write letters to *The Guardian* putting one side of the case or the other.**

Worksheet 3 Solution

1.

for Ms. Styler	against Ms. Styler
• has exposed devastation caused by Chevron • has raised millions of pounds for the Rainforest Foundation • has to fly to get to inaccessible places • has access to world leaders (to present her case) because she is so well-known • her flights pump little CO_2 into the atmosphere compared with rain forest destruction • *Guardian* attack may play into the hands of Chevron	• does do a great deal of flying (is it all really necessary?) • obviously has a rather inflated idea of her own importance – at least the *Guardian* thinks so ("madam's most cherished public pose: that of eco warrior") • does not practise what she preaches (cf. texts in the SB, p. 37–38, p. 47) • the fact that the *Guardian* article made her so angry suggests that she has a bad conscience

2.

Free activity.

Some expressions for the letter:

Sir, I was surprised/amazed/shocked/delighted to read Trudie Styler's attack on your article. I am sure that people like her are doing a wonderful job/are just full of their own importance/are not doing half as much good as they would like to think. She comes across as a sincere/hard-working/big-headed/arrogant/unpleasant person. You can see (all too clearly) that she likes being famous/really tries to make a difference. People who can't afford to fly all over the place are just jealous of people like her – and that includes your journalists! We attach too much importance to individual carbon footprints – if her activities save far more carbon than is emitted on her account, then we shouldn't complain. Good luck to her!

In future, I feel that *The Guardian* should continue to attack/be more sympathetic towards people like Trudie Styler.

Note: Letters printed in newspapers only add the writer's name (and sometimes the town s/he lives in) nowadays – no yours etc., yours faithfully/truly.

Klausur 1

Rock Battery Could Store Electricity

Danny Fortson

POWER from the wind and the sun is the future, we are told. There's just one snag[1] – these power sources aren't dependable. Unless there is a way to store electricity in times of plenty we will need a lot of back-up power, probably fossil-fuelled, to tide us over[2] when the clouds move in or the wind stops blowing. And that's not very green.
Isentropic, a five-man outfit[3] in Cambridge, thinks it has the answer: a gravel[4] battery. It may sound distinctly low-tech, but the company has come up with some clever engineering to make tanks of rocks into electricity stores. It comes from an idea pioneered in the 1830s by John Ericsson, the prolific[5] Swedish inventor who designed a hot-air engine and the USS Monitor, the ironclad[6] warship of the American civil war.
Mark Wagner, a former hedge-fund manager who is now the company's chairman, said Isentropic came about because of another boat. A sailing enthusiast, he was on the lookout for new hydrofoil[7] designs in his attempt to set a world speed record.
When he came across a novel model on the Internet, he called its designer, John Howes, an engineer at the Civil Aviation Authority. "We worked on the boat for a while, but then he told me about this heat pump he was working on." That was eight years ago.

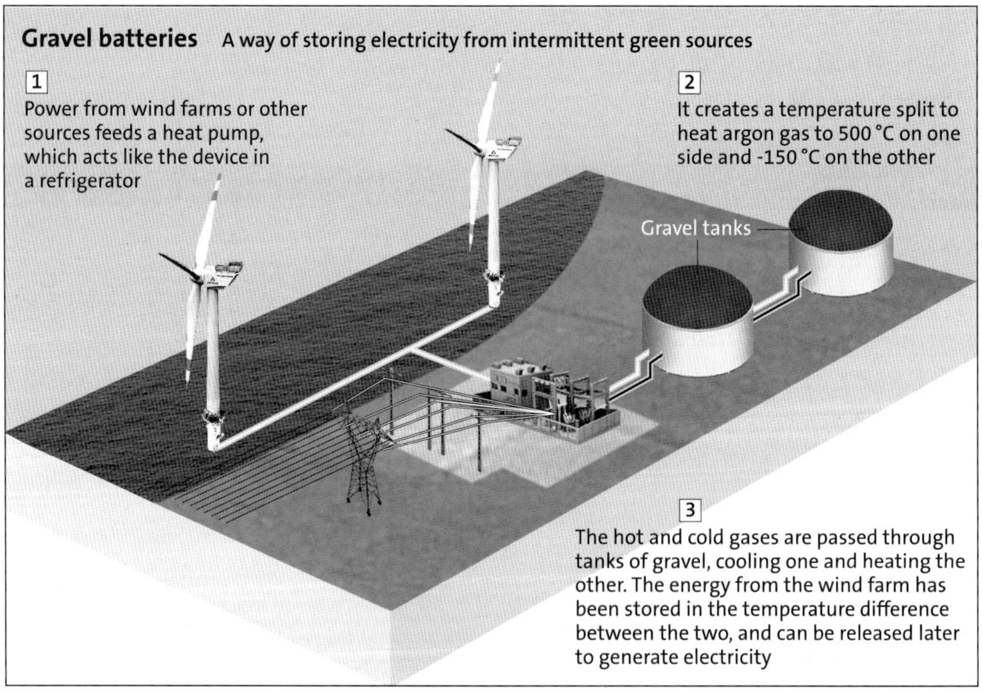

[1] **snag** hidden or unexpected difficulty
[2] **to tide sb. over** to help sb. during a difficult period
[3] **outfit** *here* a small group of people working together
[4] **gravel** small stones
[5] **prolific** producing many ideas and/or inventions
[6] **ironclad** covered by iron
[7] **hydrofoil** a device raising a boat out of the water, allowing it to travel faster

Klausur 1

Isentropic's "battery" works like this. An electrical current feeds a heat pump, a bigger version of the device that keeps your fridge cold. The fridge in your kitchen uses electricity to drive a tiny heat pump to create a temperature split, chilling the inside of the fridge and warming the back.

Isentropic's system uses Howes's pump to heat argon gas to 500°C on one side while cooling it to –150°C on the other. The hot and cold gas is then passed through two giant gravel tanks, heating one and cooling the other. The power is stored in the gravel as a temperature difference.

When power is needed, the process can be instantly reversed and the heat pump now works like an engine – the extreme temperatures are brought together and turn the engine, which powers a generator to create electricity.

Today most of the world's electricity storage systems are based on hydro-electric schemes with two reservoirs. When power is needed, water is released from the top reservoir to drive a turbine and then pass into the lower reservoir. When there is surplus[8] power, the turbine pumps water back up to the higher reservoir. The disadvantage is that it takes a huge amount of power to pump the water back up. Dinorwig hydro station in Wales is run only at times of peak demand, when prices are highest.

Wagner said his team has proved the technology with a pair of prototypes and is now looking for funding to build a demonstration plant. Between him, the other founders and a handful of private investors, they have invested about £1.5m so far. Other companies are working on a similar technology.

Danny Fortson: „Rock Battery Could Store Electricity", in: *The Sunday Times*, June 14, 2009

---

[8] **surplus** more than needed at a time

Activities

1. **Outline how gravel batteries store electricity.**
2. **Analyse the last paragraph of the article. What effect does it have on the reader?**
3. **You have a choice:**

   a) **Evaluate the importance of rock batteries/batteries for the development of alternative energy.**

   or:

   b) **Write a letter to the editor commenting on the future of rock batteries.**

Klausur 2

From the Melting Frontline, a Chilling View of a Warming World

Patrick Barkham

It is calving[1] season in the Arctic. A flotilla[2] of icebergs, some as jagged[3] as fairytale castles and others as smooth as dinosaur eggs, calve from the ice sheet that smothers[4] Greenland and sail down the fjords. The journey of these sculptures of ice from glaciers[5] to ocean is eerily[6] beautiful and utterly[7] terrifying. The wall of ice that rises behind Sermilik fjord stretches for 1,500 miles (2,400 km) from north to south and smothers 80 % of this country. It has been frozen for 3m years. Now it is melting, far faster than the climate models predicted and far more decisively than any political action to combat[8] our changing climate. If the Greenland ice sheet disappeared sea levels around the world would rise by seven metres, as 10 % of the world's fresh water is currently frozen here. This is also the season for science in Greenland. Glaciologists[9], seismologists[10] and climatologists from around the world are landing on the ice sheet in helicopters, taking ice-breakers up its inaccessible coastline and measuring glaciers in a race against time to discover why the ice in Greenland is vanishing so much faster than expected.

Gordon Hamilton, a Scottish-born glaciologist from the University of Maine's Climate Change Institute, is packing up equipment at his base camp in Tasiilaq, a tiny, remote east coast settlement only accessible by helicopter and where huskies howl all night. [...] Four years ago he hit upon[11] the daring idea of landing on a moving glacier in a helicopter to measure its speed.

The glaciers of Greenland are the fat, restless fingers of its vast[12] ice sheet, constantly moving, stretching down into fjords and pushing ice from the sheet into the ocean, in the form of melt water and icebergs.

Before their first expedition, Hamilton and his colleague Leigh Steams, from the University of Kansas, used satellite data to plan exactly where they would land on a glacier.

"When we arrived there was no glacier to be seen. It was way up the fjord," he says. "We thought we'd made some stupid goof[13] with the co-ordinates, but we were where we were supposed to be." It was the glacier that was in the wrong place. A vast expanse[14] had melted away.

---

1 **to calve** to give birth, usually used for cows
2 **flotilla** a group of ships
3 **jagged** pointed, with sharp edges
4 **to smother** to cover thickly
5 **glacier** *Gletscher*
6 **eerie** causing a feeling of mystery and fear
7 **utterly** completely
8 **to combat** to fight
9 **glaciologist** sb. who studies glaciers
10 **seismologist** sb. who studies earthquakes
11 **to hit upon sth.** to think of sth.
12 **vast** very large in area or size
13 **goof** mistake
14 **expanse** a wide area

Klausur 2

When Hamilton and Steams processed[15] their first measurements of the glacier's speed, they thought they had made another mistake. They found it was marching forwards at a greater pace[16] than a glacier had ever been observed to flow before. "We were blown away because we realised that the glaciers had accelerated not just by a little bit but by a lot," he says. The three glaciers they studied had abruptly increased the speed by which they were transmitting ice from the ice sheet into the ocean.

Patrick Barkham: "From the Melting Frontline, a Chilling View of a Warming World", in: The Guardian, September 1, 2009, p. 1, © Guardian News & Media Ltd 2009

---

[15]**to process** to analyse
[16]**pace** speed

Activities

1. **Describe the situation in the Arctic and explain what Gordon Hamilton does for a living and how he approaches this particular job.**
2. **Analyse the first paragraph. What kind of atmosphere is created and what effect does it have on the reader?**
3. **Write an interview with Gordon Hamilton focusing on what can be done "to combat our changing climate".**

Klausur 2 Solution

1. Features of the situation in the Arctic:

- 80% of the land in Greenland is covered with ice, (some of) which has been frozen for 3m. years.
- Now these glaciers are melting much faster than climate models predict.
- The glaciers contain 10% of the world's fresh water.
- If the Greenland ice sheet disappeared, sea levels would rise by 7 metres.

Gordon Hamilton's job:

- He is a glaciologist – someone who studies glaciers.
- When the glaciers start to calve, people like Hamilton arrive in Greenland to study them.
- In particular, they want to find out why the glaciers are melting so much faster than anticipated/predicted.
- Hamilton and a colleague decided to land on a glacier to carry out their studies/experiments, but found that it had retreated a long way back from the place where they had planned to land.
- They wanted to measure movement up on the glacier itself.
- They discovered that it (and other glaciers in the area) was/were moving/flowing faster than any glacier(s) had ever moved before.

2. Points which could be made:

- First few lines: very dramatic atmosphere, use of similes to reinforce this impression: 'jagged as fairytale castles', 'smooth as dinosaur eggs'.
- Sense that this scene is somehow mysterious, beyond normal experience, frightening for human beings: 'eerily beautiful', 'utterly terrifying'.
- On a vast scale: 1 500 miles long, covers 80% of the country (and Greenland is sometimes referred to as the world's largest island). The ice has been there for three million years. In other words, we are dealing with a truly enormous amount of ice, which has been fairly stable for a very long time.
- The writer is trying to get across to the reader the terrifying fact that when all this ice melts, the consequences for the world are bound to be catastrophic.
- As the paragraph continues, these consequences are outlined, and we then join the scientists who are engaged in 'a race against time' (another dramatic expression) to try to find out why the ice is melting so fast.

3. Student: Good morning, Mr Hamilton. I understand you have just returned from a rather worrying visit to Greenland.

Hamilton: Gordon, please! Yes – but I'm afraid 'rather worrying' is a bit of an understatement.

S: How do you mean?

H: Well, it's more than just worrying – terrifying is a better word, I'm afraid.

S: So just how bad is it up there in Greenland?

H: Well the glaciers are melting – and moving towards the sea – faster than ever before.

S: And this is very bad news for us, of course.

Klausur 2 Solution

H: Yes, it is. If all that ice melts, sea levels will rise by seven metres, which means that huge low-lying areas of land will be flooded, many of them densely populated. As you probably know, some groups of islands will soon have to be evacuated.
S: Yes – even London is threatened, I believe.
H: Not to mention Holland, the German west coast and so on.
S: So is there anything we can do to stop, or at least slow down the melting process?
H: Well, I'm not really the right person to ask about that – I just study the glaciers and tell people what is happening to them. But the solutions are familiar to anyone who reads the newspaper.
S: Stop burning fossil fuel, stop cutting down the rain forests, stop flying, stop driving 4x4s, tell China to stop building coal-fired power stations, re-cycle more waste, change the light bulbs ...
H: Exactly. The problem is, and this is something I really saw properly for the first time in Greenland, the melting process is on a truly enormous scale – and it's actually *accelerating* – all our efforts are not even slowing it down.
Getting it to reverse is a bit like someone trying to turn a giant container ship round by pulling on a bit of rope. I'm afraid we won't be able to do it.
S: No hope then?
H: Well, we are making some progress, at least in the old industrial countries – and the ice in the middle of Greenland is actually getting thicker – we think it's because of increased rainfall as a result of higher temperatures.
S: Fingers crossed, then?
H: Toes as well!
S: Thanks very much for the interview, Mr ... Gordon.
H: My pleasure.